On His Own Side of the Puck

The Early History of Hockey Rules

Including complete codes of hockey laws by the score and for several other nineteenth century sports including ricket, bandy, lacrosse, roller polo, field hockey (Blackheath, Eton, Association) and football (Cambridge, Sheffield, Rugby and Association)

Iain Fyffe

ISBN 978-0-9936851-1-8

DEDICATION

For my father, who gave me my
first books on hockey history

- and -

For my wife, who tolerates
all the hours I put into this

CONTENTS

PREFACE

This book contains rules, lots and lots of rules. List after endless list of rules. There's lots of discussion as well, adding context, clarification and commentary to the codes of law. To the extent possible, the full text of a set of rules is included. I believe this is important; if I give you my interpretation of a rule you should have the wording of the rule and its context to examine for yourself. How else can you decide whether my interpretation is accurate? I do not expect you to rely on my summary of a rule or set of rules; while I may provide such a summary at times, the full text is also there. This results in a good deal of repetition at times, but there is value in reproducing the full text of all the codes under discussion.

When a list of rules is provided, you'll note that each rule in the set is numbered. This numbering does not necessary correspond with the number assigned (if any) in the original text. I have kept the original ordering of rules, but at times have revised the specific numbers used, to improve clarity and consistency in presentation.

Much of this book is therefore a rather dry read, consisting of lists of rules accompanied by some commentary. Don't expect to get your heart rate up by reading this stuff. It's interesting and it's historically relevant, but it's far from exciting. No apology is made for that fact.

ACKNOWLEDGEMENTS

I would like to acknowledge the assistance of many members of the Society for International Hockey Research (SIHR), whether they realized they were providing it or not: Pat Houda, Carl Giden, J-P Martel, Lloyd Davis, Earl Zuckerman, Michel Vigneault and Craig Bowlsby, and most likely some others that I have forgotten. Thanks also to Mike Smith, curator of the National Hockey Museum in Woking, UK. But special thanks are reserved for J. W. (Bill) Fitsell, founding member and past president of SIHR, who provided a good deal of crucial information and input to this work.

PROLOGUE

Picture it: a Canadian city in the mid-1890s, at a frigid rink. Artificial ice rinks haven't been introduced yet, so the patrons are as cold as the playing surface. They're here to witness a match of that most Canadian of winter sports: hockey. The game has existed as a spectator sport for less than two decades, and for much less time than that outside of Montreal. But it has spread like wildfire, and brings thrills to the gathered masses of onlookers. The game is about to begin...

Along the sides of the rink, stand ranks of the most enthusiastic friends of the players, to applaud and encourage. In the ends of the building, on raised galleries sit scores of fair ladies wrapped in their warm furs, who show by their attendance that they admire muscular manhood. The electric and gas lights are turned on. The referee advances to the centre of the ice and the umpires take post at their respective goals. The members of the two teams...file on the field. Preliminaries are arranged. The players take their places. One player on each side faces off in the centre of the field, by having the puck placed between the flat of their respective sticks. A pause of breathless interest, and then the referee calls out: "Are you ready? - Draw!" and they are at it like a flash.

Hither and thither the rubber goes. It glides, caroms, flies, rebounds, so swiftly that its whereabouts is known half the time only by the movements of the players, who dash after it by intuition. It is suddenly lifted clear from the ice and curves swiftly toward one of the goals. If it is not checked by curved sticks raised to stop it, it may reach the goalkeeper whose knees stop it and a slash of his stick carries it off to one side. Then the point takes it in the opposite direction. In his flight he may dodge, or carom the puck, or pass it back to one of his own players if his progress is checked, but he is now virtually out of the play for the time being, because he is ahead of the puck, and cannot touch it until it has been sent on ahead of him again, and even then he cannot touch it until it has been touched by an opponent. It he is the first to reach it, he may only lay his stick behind the puck to check it instantly after the other has delivered his play.

Now one of the forwards has the puck well down upon the enemy's goal, and his dashing attack is supported by every man who can be spared, as they close in to rush it through. But there is many a slip in hockey. A foul occurs in front of the goal and there is a face off. A face off there is dangerous, and the defenders mass solidly to protect their goal. One of the attacking players faces off, the rest open up like a fan behind him, to shoot on goal if the puck comes back out of the defence. A scrimmage in front of or close to the goal is the acme of excitement. Each player strains every nerve in the attack or defence, the goalkeeper bends low, his muscles tense, his eyes following the rubber like those of a hawk. At last by a skilful sweep of the stick the goal is relieved, and the play shifts to the centre of the field, and then begins some beautiful individual and team play, as there is now scope for swift skating and artful dodging. It seems strange that men are not maimed or injured as they skim around at such a breakneck speed.

Without a moment's warning, for the unexpected always occurs, the rubber goes down upon one of the goals and is swiped between the goal posts, past the vigilant warder of the gates. Up goes the arm of the umpire and the roof of the rink rings with the cheers of friends of the victorious side, who wave their sticks in the air in sympathy with the applause. There is a rest of a few minutes, and then play is resumed after the goal keepers have exchanged ends. And so it goes until the last goal is scored and the star player of the victors is borne from the ice upon the shoulders of his admirers.

(From Woodside, H.J. "Hockey in the Canadian North-West." *The Canadian Magazine* VI.3 (1896): 242-247.)

Chapter One

THE MEANING OF HOCKEY

What defines a game if not its rules? Without rules to delineate your activity, you cannot say you're playing hockey while another plays bandy; you're both simply hitting a thing with a stick on the ice. Rules define what a game is, and what it is not. No conversation about what hockey is can be had without reference to its rules.

Indeed, an organized game of any kind cannot exist without rules; it would not be organized if there were no code of laws governing its play. In discussing the origins of hockey, lack of specificity about the organization and rules of the game often leads to confusion. The meaning of the simple word "hockey" has changed a good deal over time, yet most writers use it without qualification, even when using it in a historical context. The original meaning was basically an activity that involves hitting a ball or other small object with a stick. This has changed over time to its current meaning, which (in North America at least) is narrowly construed to mean only a specific type of that game, as played in the National Hockey League and many other leagues.

When one is discussing these things in a historical context, one must be careful to define terms carefully to avoid talking past others, who may mean something different by the term being used. If someone writes "hockey's origins are in Montreal in the 1870s", they clearly do not mean hockey in the older sense of the activity of hitting a thing with a stick. As such, a response that points out there are centuries-old illustrations of hockey in Europe is an invalid rebuttal to the point, as this response does not use the same definition of the word hockey.

It is therefore crucial to define exactly what you mean by the word hockey, when you use it in a particular context. For clarity, in this book I will use the term "organized hockey" to mean the current version of the game we know and love, and the forms that we know led directly to it, and I will use the term "informal hockey", if needed, to describe previous versions of the game, before it was organized. I hope to avoid confusion in this way.

1

In order to discuss the origins of the rules of organized hockey, clearly we first need to establish what elements need to be present in order for the game to be recognizable as such. These elements need to be general enough to include the current version of what we call hockey, while also including the game from, say, 1928 when the forward passing rules were quite different, or from 1910 when the game still included the rover position. But these elements also need to be specific enough to exclude other similar games, such as bandy or shinny. Bandy in its current form is recognizably different from contemporary organized hockey, so its definition must be distinct from that of organized hockey.

In the first significant book about ice hockey, *Hockey: Canada's Royal Winter Game* (1899), Montreal Shamrocks star and then-future Hall-of-Famer Art Farrell quotes *Webster's Dictionary* in defining the game of hockey as it was in 1899:

"[Hockey is a] game in which two parties of players, armed with sticks or clubs, curved or hooked at the end, attempt to drive any small object (as a ball or a bit of wood) towards opposite goals."

But this definition is clearly not suitable for our purposes, and indeed Farrell notes that this definition seems to refer to the English version of the game, which we call field hockey. Really it defines the general activity of hockey, not the specific organized version we are interested in, or indeed any organized version of the activity. We can, however, adapt this definition to arrive at the meaning of organized hockey:

Organized hockey is a competitive game that is played using a codified set of rules on an enclosed ice rink in which two teams of players wearing skates and using sticks that are curved at the end, attempt to propel a puck though their opponents' goal, with the number of goals so scored by each team being used to determine the result of the match.

Two crucial elements in this definition are often overlooked when discussing hockey's origins: the skates and the puck. Hockey is not organized hockey without skates, though some writers are all too eager to call any game played on ice to be equivalent to organized hockey, without qualification. The puck is equally important to the definition of organized hockey, and equally overlooked. There must be a puck for it to be organized hockey; otherwise you will have difficulty in differentiating the game from bandy or the nineteenth century game of ice polo, both of which use balls. Without the puck/ball distinction, you would need to get into more minute details to separate these games, such as the size of the rink or the shape of the sticks, or the number of players on each team or the degree to which body contact is allowed. Using such details to make the definition is not desirable, because they have changed over the life of what we want to include in organized hockey. They therefore should not be used as defining characteristics.

For instance, bandy is played on a rink that is between two-and-a-half and four-and-a-half times the area of a standard North American hockey rink. If it were played on a smaller rink, would it become hockey instead? If so, at what point would this occur? Similarly, if organized hockey were played on a larger rink, would it become bandy? Organized hockey hasn't always been played on a standard-sized rink; many rinks used for high-level organized hockey in the past have been significantly smaller than the current standard, which is based on the dimensions of the Victoria Skating Rink in Montreal. So the specific size of the rink can't be used in the definition of organized hockey. A similar problem would exist by using the specific shape of the stick; the sticks used in early organized hockey look more like modern bandy sticks that they do modern hockey sticks. Fortunately, there is a distinguishing feature available for use in our definition: the puck.

The puck is the greatest innovation of organized hockey. Early organized hockey, when it was praised, was praised for its science. An archaic term when used in this context, science here means play that is planned, deliberate, intricate, and coordinated. A forward line rushing with the puck, executing quick, accurate passes to advance is an example of scientific hockey. There is an argument to be made that this science is what promoted the rapid growth of organized hockey in

Canada. And this level of science in the game was made possible by the introduction of the puck.

As we'll see in Chapter Two, the puck was invented for the purpose of spectator safety. In informal hockey, a ball was generally used for the game. A round ball on ice is clearly prone to a terrible amount of bouncing around. Passing the ball to a teammate accurately must have been a very difficult task, and the game would have involved a lot of back-and-forth as everyone tries to gain control of the unruly object. On the other hand, a puck can slide along the ice, enabling accurate passing and shooting which allows much more science to be brought into the game. Of course, even with a puck there is a good deal of chaos in the game, especially in olden times when the ice was generally more uneven and choppy, but it's all relative.

The *Montreal Gazette* of March 17, 1875, in covering only the second recorded game of organized hockey, noted that James Creighton's team played with a great deal of "science" and that early on they had an "organized system" which distinguished their play. Such systematic play was characteristic of onside combination play in early organized hockey, rather than a strategy of relying on individual rushes without much passing. With scientific combination play, when advancing the puck a team passes the puck amongst themselves, using short, quick passes to confound the defence.

Farrell (1899) wrote that organized hockey is "the most fascinating, the most exciting, the most scientific" of all games, and that over time "science in play developed apace with the interest that the sport evoked." He also refers to organized hockey as "our glorious scientific game" and draws an explicit line between organized hockey and its predecessors when he refers to shinny as "the forerunner of our scientific hockey". Clearly, the science of the game has long been seen as a crucial factor in the great interest the sport gained in Canada.

Farrell believed that if the game had not been organized, its popularity would not be what it was:

"Twenty-five years ago [i.e., 1874], *hockey, as played to-day* [i.e., organized hockey], *was an unknown sport. Shinny was played on the lakes, rivers and canals throughout the country, but only a discerning eye could discover in this crude, but infatuating amusement, the grand possibilities that a refined game could offer. Without restrictions as to the proportions of the stick, the nature or quality of the puck, the size of the playing space on the ice, or the number of the players, the sport could not develop into a scientific game, until such time as it would be discussed and regulated, by those who sought its advancement."*
(Farrell 1899, p. 27)

Key among the rules of this new organized game was the introduction of the puck, which allowed much more science into the game that would otherwise have been possible.

Kevin Allen, in *Total Hockey* (1998), describes how in 1895, a series of matches between Canadian and American teams took place, alternating between organized hockey and ice polo, a similar game that was very popular in the United States at the time. The Canadian teams had the better of the results by a good margin, and the Americans not only realized that the players from North of the border were superior in play, but that the game they played was superior as well. This was the beginning of the end for ice polo, and was the genesis of the popularity of organized hockey in the US, which grew quickly from there.

Why did organized hockey overtake ice polo so quickly? What did organized hockey have that ice polo did not? The puck, of course. In *How Hockey Happened* (2006), J.W. (Bill) Fitsell quotes the editor of the 1886 edition of *Henley's Official Polo Guide*, referring to roller polo, from which the ice version derived:

"Polo should be played by keeping the ball as much as possible on the surface, not driving it through the air as in shinny or baseball...Keeping it upon the floor makes a better and more interesting game, and requires more skill, ability and judgment."

"Skill, ability and judgment" is of course a good definition of "science" in the game as we've been discussing. Thus polo experts realized that the greater control the players could exert over the ball, the better the game. Thus, when the Canadian game with its sliding puck was compared to ice polo with its bouncing ball, the preference was clear.

So this may be the great accident of organized hockey: an innovation that was intended to protect spectators from harm allowed the game to gain the degree of science that ultimately allowed its popularity to soar and spread across Canada, and beyond.

Chapter Two

THE FIRST RULES OF ORGANIZED HOCKEY

Of all the factors included in the definition of organized hockey arrived at in Chapter One, this book focuses on but one: the codified set of rules.

You're likely familiar with the official NHL rules, which for the 2012/13 season (for example) comprised 87 rules in over 120 pages of text. Most of us are also aware of many of the rule changes the NHL has undergone in its near century of existence. But in this book we're going back more than 40 years before the NHL was founded; we want to travel to the beginnings of organized hockey, to examine where its rules came from and how they developed in the early years of the game.

This, of course, means we're going back to 1875 in Montreal. The first game of organized hockey that we have record of was played on March 3rd of that year, between two nine-man teams captained by Montrealer Charles Torrance and Haligonian James Creighton respectively, the latter of which led his team to victory in a close-fought match. Mister Creighton is the key man here, one whose importance to the early development of organized hockey in Canada likely cannot be overstated. He is now generally credited with the organization of the game, and was inducted into the Nova Scotia Sport Hall of Fame in 1993 for that reason.

It is unknown, however, exactly what set of rules were used for this first game, or for the second game played later that same month. We do not have any direct references to the rules. However, we do know they used a puck. The *Montreal Gazette* of March 4, 1875 reported:

"Hockey is played usually with a ball, but last night, in order that no accident should happen, a flat block of wood was used so that it should slide along the ice without rising, and thus going among the spectators to their discomfort. The game is like Lacrosse [sic] *in one sense – the block having to go through flags placed about 8 feet apart*

The 'Rideau Hall Rebels' hockey team, c.1890. James Creighton is fourth from the left, wearing a cap. Edward and Arthur Stanley, sons of the donor of the greatest prize in hockey, are second and third from the left respectively.

in the same manner as the rubber ball – but in the main the old country game of shinty gives the best idea of hockey."

The game report in the March 17, 1875 edition of the same paper specifies that the puck was a "little circle of wood", indicating that it had a flat, circular shape. Other than the material from which it was made, it was very similar to what we now know as a puck. This is a crucial bit of information, since the presence of a puck is key in defining the game as organized hockey.

As we'll see, with respect to the origin of the uncertain rules used in these two games, a great deal of importance is to be placed on whether this game was played using some kind of offside rule. In its essential form, an offside rule states that a player who is ahead of the puck or ball (that is, closer to his opponent's end than the puck or ball is) is out of play. Such a rule does not allow forward passing, in the sense of passing the object to a player closer to the opponent's goal than you are.

This first game report does not specify whether the game was an onside one or not. The references to lacrosse and shinty, neither of which were onside games, might suggest that the game played that day also was not. However, the report also points out that the game was unfamiliar to Montreal, and as such presumably the author of the report had limited experience with it as well, so something as specific as an offside rule may not have been deemed important enough for inclusion in the brief report, and may not have been noticed at all. And given what we know about the laws of the game used in 1876 and 1877, both of which include an offside rule as we'll see, it seems quite unlikely that they played their first game without an offside rule and then decided to add one, considering how persistent the rule was after that time.

As noted in the *Montreal Gazette* of March 15, 1875, one of the teams to play that night, captained by James Creighton was selected from among the Montreal Football Club members. In fact, seven of the eight Football Club members that played that night (George Campbell, Stewart Campbell, William Chapman, Edward Clouston, Robert Esdaile, Fred Henshaw and Henry Joseph) also played with Creighton in the very first recorded game. Football (whether soccer or rugby) was, of course, an onside game. The fact that all of these players were used to an onside game suggest that the organized hockey they played was also probably onside.

The *Montreal Gazette* of February 7, 1876 contains the first reference to an actual set of rules that were used in the third recorded game of organized hockey, reporting that the game "was conducted under the 'Hockey Association' rules." We will address the Hockey Association in more detail in Chapter Four. Finally, a report in the February 27, 1877 edition of the same paper finally provided complete details of the rules themselves. These rules have since become known as the Montreal Rules, and are as follows:

The Montreal Rules - 1877

Rule 1: The game shall be commenced and renewed by a Bully in the centre of the ground. Goals [ends] shall be changed after each game [goal].

Rule 2: When a player hits the ball, any one of the same side who at such moment of hitting is nearer to the opponents' goal line is out of play, and may not touch the ball himself, or in any way whatever prevent any other player from doing so, until the ball has been played. A player must always be on his own side of the ball.

Rule 3: The ball may be stopped, but not carried or knocked on by any part of the body. No player shall raise his stick above his shoulder. Charging from behind, tripping, collaring [grabbing the sweater], kicking or shinning [slashing on the shins] shall not be allowed.

Rule 4: When the ball is hit behind the goal line by the attacking side, it shall be brought out straight 15 yards, and started again by a Bully; but, if hit behind by any one of the side whose goal line it is, a player of the opposite side shall hit it out from within one yard of the nearest corner, no player of the attacking side at that time shall be within 20 yards of the goal line, and the defenders, with the exception of the goal-keeper, must be behind their goal line.

Rule 5: When the ball goes off at the side, a player of the opposite side to that which hit it out shall roll it out from the point on the boundary line at which it went off at right angles with the boundary line, and it shall not be in play until it has touched the ice, and the player rolling it in shall not play it until it has been played by another player, every player being then behind the ball.

Rule 6: On the infringement of any of the above rules, the ball shall be brought back and a Bully shall take place.

Rule 7: All disputes shall be settled by the Umpires, or in the event of their disagreement, by the Referee.

Note that these rules refer to a ball rather than a puck. This is because they are an edited version of English field hockey rules, as we'll see later. The fact that these rules say "ball" rather than "puck" does, however, strongly suggest that these rule predate the first game of organized hockey in 1875. Creighton and his mates seem to have settled upon the rules before deciding that a ball would not be used. As such, these rules appear to predate the first recorded match on March 3, 1875. Note that the writers of these rules did change references from "ground" to "ice", so if they were already using something other than a ball when they were written, the references to "ball" would most likely have been changed as well. This is not conclusive, but is certainly suggestive that these were the rules from the beginning of organized hockey in 1875.

We'll be exploring these rules in more detail, especially where they came from, in Chapter Four. Before that, however, we need to get one thing out of the way. There is one fairly common suggestion for the origin of these rules, which we'll call the Halifax Hypothesis, which needs to be addressed.

Chapter Three

THE HALIFAX HYPOTHESIS

There is one proposed explanation of the origins of the first organized hockey rules, which is based on the fact that James Creighton, the organizer of the game himself, was born in Halifax, Nova Scotia in 1850. He moved to Montreal in 1872, only three years before the first game of organized hockey. The best sticks and skates in the world at the time were known to come from Halifax. As such, the rules of organized hockey must also have come from Halifax, and Creighton simply imported to Montreal the rules he had been using back home for years. These suggestions are related to the various "Nova Scotia is the one and only true birthplace of hockey" claims, such as those put forward by the late Garth Vaughan in his book *The Puck Starts Here* and the website *The Birthplace of Hockey*® (emphasis in original).

Unfortunately for the Halifax Hypothesis, the so-called Halifax Rules were never committed to writing, at least in a form that has survived to today. No reference to a contemporary written version of these rules has been found either. Vaughan's site does list a set of purported rules, which were based on the recollections of one Byron Weston, who lived in Dartmouth, Nova Scotia in the 1860s, and related them to writer James Power of the *Halifax Herald*. These are also referenced by Bill Fitsell in a *Hockey Research Journal* article related to the Halifax Rules (Fitsell 2001).

The Halifax Rules, as recorded by James Power in 1943, are as follows:

The "Halifax Rules" - allegedly 1860s

Rule 1: The game was played with a block of wood for a puck.

Rule 2: The puck was not allowed to leave the ice.

Rule 3: The stones marking the place to score goals were placed on the ice (at right angles to those at present) parallel to the sides of the ice surface.

Rule 4: There was to be no slashing.

Rule 5: There was to be no lifting the stick above the shoulder.

Rule 6: When a goal was scored, teams changed ends.

Rule 7: Players had to keep 'on side' of the puck.

Rule 8: The 'forward pass' was permitted.

Rule 9: All players played the entire game.

Rule 10: There was a no-replacement rule for penalized players.

Rule 11: The game had two thirty minute periods with a ten minute break.

Rule 12: The goal-keeper had to stand for the entire game.

Rule 13: Goals were decided by the goal umpires, who stood at the goal mouth and rang a handbell.

Of course, if these rules are referring to how hockey was played in Halifax in the 1860s, we're dealing with memories that were at least 74 years old when they were recorded. So they should be taken with at least a grain of salt. No offence is intended toward Mr. Weston, it's a simple fact that human memory is very fallible, much more so than most people realize. Also, there are some points in these purported rules that suggest they are not accurate on the whole.

Rule 1 refers to a block of wood being used for a puck, but the *Montreal Gazette* report states that hockey was normally played with a ball at the time. Now, it is possible that this was referring to hockey as it was played in Montreal, but the report also states that the game was not really played in that city before it was organized. Also the 1876 *Gazette* report is the first recorded use of the word "puck" to describe the disc used in a game of hockey. If a puck was in use in the 1860s in Halifax, we'd expect to see a reference to it there at some point. The reason given for creating the puck was for the safety of the spectators.

The presence of spectators implies organization, which we know (in our context) originated in Montreal in 1875. As such Rule 1 is possibly apocryphal, which suggests the same about about Rule 2, which also refers to a puck. Rule 11 and Rule 13 are also both characteristic of organized games, rather than recreation on a frozen pond.

More importantly, Rule 7 and Rule 8 are apparently contradictory. If players had to keep "on side" of the puck (Rule 7), then forward passing (Rule 8) cannot also be permitted. There cannot be a forward pass if there is no player ahead of the puck to receive it. This blatant contradiction should be enough to call into question the accuracy of the entirety of this purported code of rules; we cannot know which bits are accurate and which are not.

While it is possible that this reference to "onside" was meant to be a reference to striking the puck from only one side of a player's body (ie, a player must "shinny on his own side", a common rule in early field hockey), the wording suggests this is not the case. It does not refer to striking the puck, but its players having to remain onside.

There is evidence that some of these rules are accurate, at least in the 1880s if not the 1860s. In 1889 the Old Chebuctos club of Dartmouth travelled to Quebec to play hockey matches against some teams there. They played a total of four matches against clubs from Montreal and Quebec City, half under their own rules and half under Montreal rules, losing all of them and being outscored 23 to 3 in aggregate. In *La Coupe a Quebec* (2012), Marc Durand reports some of the differences between the two sets of rules, including that forward passing was allowed (Weston's Rule 8), that there was no lifting of the puck (Rule 2), and that the goal posts were in a different alignment (Rule 3).

Also, according to Kevin Slater (2012), in an 1887 match in Kingston, Ontario, the offside rule was experimented with but then dropped in the second half of a match *"to simplify matters and to accommodate the players who hailed from...Nova Scotia, where forward passing was allowed."* This is further evidence that Halifax hockey did not have an offside rule.

14

The Dartmouth Old Chebuctos in 1888.

Even if Weston's reported rules were completely accurate, though, it
still does not demonstrate that the first organized games of hockey in
Montreal used them. In 1876 we know Creighton and his chums were
using Hockey Association rules, meaning the rules of English field
hockey, adapted to ice. Fitsell (2001) points out that a December 1,
1877 report in McGill's school paper *The Gazette* notes that in a
Montreal match against McGill, Creighton "distinguished" himself by
playing offside early in the game. It does make sense that a man who
learned a version of the game in Halifax would play offside out of habit,
since based on what we know of the Halifax rules, there was no

offside rule. However this also cements the fact that an onside version of the game was being played in Montreal.

One version of the Halifax Hypothesis admits that the Montreal rules were based on (English) field hockey rules, but that the transition took place in Halifax before Creighton took them to Montreal. As we'll see, though, what is claimed about the content of the Halifax rules does not align well with the rules of field hockey, which in turn had been derived from association football rules. It seems far more likely that these Halifax rules, which we know did exist in some respect by at least the 1880s, were instead derived from the earlier game of ricket.

The rules of this latter game, reported to have been played in Halifax for decades before, were printed in a November 1859 edition of the *Boston Evening Gazette*. As reproduced in Fitsell (2006), they were as follows:

The Rules of Ricket - 1859

Rule 1: The rickets, or goals, consist of two cobble stones formed at one distance from another.

Rule 2: The sides are formed by two persons tossing or drawing lots for first choice of partners...until a sufficient number is obtained on each side.

Rule 3: Any number may play - "the more the merrier."

Rule 4: Each ricketer is provided with a hurley (stick.)

Rule 5: All being ready, a ball is thrown in the air.

Rule 6: A ricket (goal) is chosen by each side and placed in charge of a man whose duty it is to prevent the ball from passing through.

Rule 7: The game may be 10, 15 or 20, or any number agreed upon, the side counting the number first being winners.

Rule 8: The counting consists in putting the ball through your adversary's ricket (goal), each time counting one.

Rule 9: From the moment the ball touches the ice...it must not be taken in hand...but must be carried or struck about the ice with the hurlies.

Rule 10: Whenever the ball is put through the ricket (goal) a shout "game ho!" resounds from shore to shore.

These rules are quite sparse, but the lack of a rule prohibiting offside suggests that there was none, meaning that unlimited forward passing was allowed. These rules do not specify the alignment of the goals, but Fitsell does indicate that ricket goals were placed in the same manner as in the Halifax rules, parallel to the sides of the playing area rather than to the ends. These similarities suggest that ricket, rather than field hockey, led to the development of the Halifax Rules. This, in turn, renders it very unlikely that the Halifax Rules were used by Creighton in Montreal. The Montreal Rules were clearly based directly on field hockey, not ricket, as we'll see in Chapter Four. This problem is glossed over by Halifax Hypothesis apologists: Montreal did not allow forward passing and Halifax did, but they claim that Montreal is based on Halifax. It's an untenable argument.

Chapter Four

THE HOCKEY ASSOCIATION

So if the Montreal Rules were not based on Halifax rules, where did they come from? We know of the 1876 reference to the 'Hockey Association' code, which does not refer to any ice hockey association in Canada. It refers to the first version of the Hockey Association in England, which was formed in 1875 as an association of field hockey clubs all using a particular set of rules.

Field hockey was quite a popular game in England, which like football had many variations and no standardization before the 1860s. The Blackheath & Old Elthamians Hockey Club was formed in 1861 and developed its own code of rules, which is the first instance of a recorded set of hockey rules that we have today. We do not have a copy of the rules from 1861; the earliest extant Blackheath code is from 1863, and is reproduced below.

Blackheath Rules – 1863
Source: Giden, Carl and Pat Houda (2010). Timeline - Stick and Ball Games. Society for International Hockey Research/Swedish Ince Hockey Historical and Statistical Society.

Rule 1: Sides to be chosen as soon as ten members are present, the players' names to be written as chosen, on a paper numbered and headed Red and Blue. Anyone coming on the ground after this play has commenced, to take the first unappropriated number. Choice of goals to be decided by tossing.

Rule 2: The goal-posts to be 10 yards apart and the distance between the goals not less than 200 yards. A flag to be erected half-way.

Rule 3: Hit-off to be 50 yards out of goal, the ball to be hit from the ground. No goal can be obtained by first hit-off.

Rule 4: A player making a catch can make his mark and retire not more than four paces, and can either hit from the ground or the hand; no opponent to interfere or overstep the mark till the ball has been hit at.

Rule 5: No player shall be allowed to loiter within 49 yards of the goal of the opposite side unless the ball be between him and his opponents goal.

Rule 6: After a goal has been obtained the sides shall change their respective goals, the winning side to hit-off.

Rule 7: The ball shall not be taken off the ground so long as it is in play; except it pass by the goal-posts; the striker shall then have the same privilege as in Rule 4.

Rule 8: The ball shall not be in play when outside he boundary flags, and is then to be tossed on straight by the nearest player, but shall not be in play till it has touched the ground within bounds.

Rule 9: It shall be a goal if the ball pass through the goals, or above the space between them, provided it does not pass over a cross-pole. A goal may be saved by a catch within the poles.

Several of these rules are confirmed by Nevill Miroy in his *The History of Hockey* (1986). Miroy also notes that the norm was 15 players per side (goalkeeper, two backs, two three-quarter backs, three half backs and seven forwards), and that left-handed hitting was outlawed in 1863. This was a common restriction in early hockey games, sometimes worded that a player must shinny on his own side, and was designed to prevent collisions between players of opposite sides who were both trying for the ball. According to the source above, however, this rule did not enter the Blackheath code until 1870.

Miroy also points out that the "ball" used in the Blackheath rules was actually a rubber cube weighing no more than seven ounces, which had to be boiled regularly to maintain its elasticity. Smith and Robson however, in their 1899 book *Hockey Historical and Practical* point out that a rubber cube was not always used in the Blackheath game:

"For many years a ball composed of a bung [ie, a stopper for a barrel], *a piece of cork or a piece of wood covered with string, and generally about the size of a cricket-ball (or, if anything, rather larger), was used by the clubs throughout the country; and even after the National*

Union was formed [in 1887] *the used of this ball was still in vogue, as it was difficult to obtain the solid cube of india-rubber which the London Club* [apparently a reference to Blackheath, which is part of London County] *had adopted in its early days."* (Smith and Robson, p.16)

Smith and Robson also claim that left-handed hitting was always disallowed in the Blackheath version of the game, which is not included in the list of laws above. This does not appear to be accurate.

Almost none of these rules have any relevance to the Montreal Rules. It does contain an offside rule of sorts (Rule 5), but it is really more of a historical curiosity from the perspective of organized hockey rules. Although it predates the Hockey Association code by over a decade, it did not have a lasting direct impact outside of the Blackheath club and other clubs that used the same rules.

Another, much more detailed version of field hockey rules were developed at Eton College, and published in 1868.

Eton Hockey Rules
Source: Eton College Chronicle, 20 Feb 1868.

Rule 1: The Ground is 200 yards long, and 50 yards broad, marked out by sticks.

Rule 2: At the distance of 20 yards from the line of the goal sticks two sticks are placed along the side line, one on each side of the ground. These are called "Lamming Sticks."

Rule 3: Goals sticks are placed at each end, 20 feet apart, and 7 feet high.

Rule 4: The sticks used may be according to the fancy of each player, as long as it is recognized as fair by the Keepers. No player may have more than one stick in his hand at a time.

Rule 5: A large sized tennis-ball is used.

Rule 6: The two sides do consist of 11 players each: there being two "Guards" and one "Goal-keeper" to each side. The rest forming the "Bully."

Rule 7: A "Bully" is formed by each side being drawn up in a long line in the direction of the length of the ground, having their right hands towards their own goals: the ball being places between the sticks of the middle player on each side.

Rule 8: No player is allowed to raise his stick above the knee, except when inside the "Lamming Sticks," when he may hit as hard as he likes, due regard to safety being had.

Rule 9: The stick must be held on the right side of the player, and the ball struck at with it in that position, in order that all collision of bodies and rouging [sic] be avoided.

Rule 10: If any player violating this rule impedes his adversary he can with impunity be struck on the shin.

Rule 11: The ball may be stopped, but not kicked with the foot.

Rule 12: The ball may be stopped in the air with the hand, but not held.

Rule 13: Any player violating the above two rules to leave the ball alone until it has been touched by an adversary.

Rule 14: It is the duty of the two "Guards" to stand outside the Bully, and endeavour to keep the ball in the middle of the ground, and to prevent any adversary from passing them with it; also to prevent "sneaking."

Rule 15: No player may "corner" or "sneak." [neither of these terms are defined in the rules]

Rule 16: On any player violating the above rule, any one of the opposing party may claim a Bully at the spot where the offence was committed.

Rule 17: Play lasts an hour, and is commenced by a Bully in the middle.

Rule 18: Goals are changed at the half-hour.

Rule 19: If the ball goes out of bounds, a Bully is formed opposite to where it went out.

Rule 20: A goal is obtained when the ball passes between the Goal Sticks, provided that the Striker be inside "Lamming Sticks."

Rule 21: If the ball pass between the Goal Sticks, struck from beyond the "Lamming Sticks," it counts only a "Behind."

Rule 22: If the ball passes on either side of the Goal, when struck from within "Lamming Sticks," a "behind is counter." [sic]

Rule 23: If the ball goes behind, when struck from beyond Lamming Sticks, there is a Hit-off.

Rule 24: When a Behind is obtained, a Bully is formed in front of goals at 10 yards distance from them.

Rule 25: The Striker-off is at liberty to throw the ball up for a half volley is he pleases, or to strike it in the air or on the ground.

Rule 26: No player of the adverse side may come within 20 yards of the Striker-off.

Rule 27: After a Goal, play is resumed by a Bully in the middle.

Rule 28: The Game is decided by the number of Goals each side has obtained.

Rule 29: The Game cannot be ended until the Ball has crossed the side line.

Rule 30: In the absence of Umpires, the Captain of each side acts as Umpire for his own side, and his decision is final.

It was not these rules either that were adopted by the Hockey Association. The Teddington Cricket Club formed a hockey team in 1871 and began to devise its own rules, using a cricket ball and based on the Association Football rules. The Teddington rules were certainly influenced by the Eton rules, or perhaps by the same source that the

Eton rules were derived from.

The Eton code prescribes a longer field and wider goals, but there a many similarities with the later Hockey Association rules. The lamming sticks in Rule 2 (lamming being an archaic term for striking) create a maximum distance from which a goal can be scored, there are 11 players per side (Rule 6), there is a restriction on how high the stick can be raised (Rule 8), the play must be from the right side (Rule 9), a player can stop the ball with his body but cannot play the ball with it (Rule 11 and Rule 12), a bully is taken when there is a rules infraction (Rule 16), and the goals are changed at the half (Rule 18). All of these characteristics are shared with the Hockey Association rules.

Rule 10 is very interesting, as it gives a player the power to enforce the rules directly on an opponent who has infringed them, by smacking the offender on the shins with his stick. So when the Hockey Association rules ban shinning, they're not simply referring to unintentional slashing, but the practice of players enforcing the rules through the use of violence.

When the Hockey Association was formed in 1875, its rules were based on those of the Teddington club, sometimes also called the Surbiton Rules (Channon 2012). Miroy (1986) points out that in the mid-1870s the Surbiton hockey club was playing many matches with other clubs, while Teddington was not, so perhaps it is only natural that Surbiton eventually became the side most associated with these rules. Smith and Robson (1899) instead attribute these rules to the club of East Surrey, which is geographically very close to Teddington and Surbiton, so it would be unsurprising if the rules used were the same. Miroy indicates that Blackheath was invited to join this first iteration of the Hockey Association, but the club felt their rules were "totally different", and thus declined.

Channon suggests that the Hockey Association rules were based on the Football Association rules, however it seems that the Eton rules were more important, except of course for one key rule. We will discuss the football connection in Chapter Five.

We know that the rules of the Hockey Association form the basis of the original Montreal Rules published in 1877. Looking at the Hockey Association code, we see this basis is not simply in the sense of being an inspiration, but in the very direct sense that the writers of the Montreal Rules took a copy of the Hockey Association rules and edited them to fit their game to be played on ice.

Hockey Association Rules - 1875
Source: Miroy (1986).

Rule 1: The maximum length of the ground shall be 150 yards, and the minimum length shall be 100 yards; the maximum breadth of the ground shall be 80 yards, and the minimum breadth shall be 50 yards. The length and breadth shall be marked off with flags, and the goals shall be upright posts six yards apart, with a tape across them seven feet from the ground.

Rule 2: The sticks used shall be curved wooden ones approved by the committee of the Association. The ball shall be an ordinary sized cricket ball.

Rule 3: The game shall be commenced and renewed by a bully in the centre of the ground. Goals shall be changed at half-time only.

Rule 4: When the ball is hit behind the goal-line by the attacking side, it shall be brought out straight 15 yards and started again by a bully; but if hit behind by one of the side whose goal-line it is, a player of the opposite side shall hit it out from one yard of the nearest corner flag-post, and no player shall be allowed within 20 yards of the ball until hit out.

Rule 5: When the ball is in touch, a player of the opposite side to that which hit it out shall roll it in from a point on the boundary line where it left the ground in a direction at right angles with the boundary line at least 10 yards, and it shall not be in play until it has touched the ground, and the player rolling it in shall not play it until it has been played by another player, every player being then behind the ball.

Rule 6: When a player hits the ball, and one of the same side who at such moment of hitting is nearer to the opponents' goal-line is out of play, and may not touch the ball himself, not in any way whatever prevent any other player from doing so, until the ball has been played, unless there are at least three of his opponents nearer their own goal-line; but no player is out of play when the ball is hit from the goal-line.

Rule 7: The ball may be stopped but not carried or knocked on by any part of the body. No player shall raise his stick above his shoulder. The ball shall be played from right to left, and no left or back-handed play, charging, tripping, collaring, kicking or shinning be allowed.

Rule 8: To obtain a goal a player must hit the ball between the posts and under the tape.

Rule 9: No goal shall be allowed if the ball be hit from a distance of more than 15 yards from the nearest goal-posts.

Rule 10: In all cases of a bully, every player shall be behind the ball.

Rule 11: On the infringement of any of the above rules, the ball shall be brought back and a bully shall take place.

Rule 12: The ordinary number of players shall be eleven a side.

We can clearly see the Montreal Rules buried in there. James Creighton and his compatriots did a bit more than simply changing "ground" to "ice", but they clearly started with this set of rules, and kept much of the exact wording. Rule 1 and Rule 2 were omitted, which is understandable given they were playing only at one rink at the time, and their sticks were imported, meaning selection was probably limited anyway. More importantly, there was no association in existence to approve a stick for use in the game. Similar rules to these two were eventually added, in 1893 and 1886 respectively. Rule 8 and Rule 9 were also omitted, the former likely being seen as self-evident (and later being added to the organized hockey code in 1886), and the latter simply not being used, and has indeed never been used in ice hockey. Rule 11, setting out the number of players, was not considered in the earliest Montreal Rules; teams had some flexibility in the number of players in a game until the 1886 rules, when it was limited to seven aside. Rule 3 was adapted by changing the frequency at which goals were alternated. Rule 4, Rule 5 and Rule 11 were transferred verbatim.

The key offside rule, Rule 6, was imported almost word-for-word into the Montreal Rules, but had the end bit cut off, removing the exception when there are a certain number of defenders between the player and the goal. Also added was the statement that players must always be on their own side of the puck, which, since the offside exception was not included, does nothing to really change the rules but does clarify them. The other important decision made by the crafters of the first Montreal Rules was to not import the field hockey requirement from Rule 7 to play right-handed only, and to play the ball only from right to left. That is to say, in organized hockey, a player did not have to shinny on his own side.

One might question the direct lineage of the first rules of organized hockey, given the timing. The Hockey Association was not formed until 1875, the same year that the first organized hockey match was played. Can we accept that the code of field hockey laws crossed the Atlantic so quickly? In fact we can, since we know that the Hockey Association adopted an existing set of rules when it was formed; it did not create a new code. Arlott (1977) confirms that the Teddington Club rules predate the Hockey Association. The oldest surviving minute book from the Teddington Club is from 1874, and Arlott notes that in that year the club amended one of the existing rules to read "*A player may not stop the ball with his hand, not shall he, in any case, raise his stick above his shoulder...*" which should seem familiar given the 1877 Montreal Rules.

Moreover, we know that much of the Teddington code was not created by that club. The April 1862 edition of *Every Boy's Magazine*, published in London, contained an article by John George Wood (writing under the name George Forrest) about the game of hockey for boys. This article included a list of eight rules, many of which will seem very familiar when compared to the Hockey Association code.

Boys' Hockey Rules - 1862
Source: Forrest, George (1862). "Hockey" in Every Boy's Magazine *No. 3, London: Routledge, Warne and Routledge.*

Rule 1: The game is won by the ball passing through the enemy's goal.

Rule 2: The ball must be struck through the goal with the stick, not thrown or kicked.

Rule 3: Each player shall strike from right to left, and any played infringing this rule is liable to the penalty of a blow on the shins from any of the opposite side.

Rule 4: Each player shall remain on his own side, and if he crosses to that of the opponents is liable to the same penalty.

Rule 5: No player shall raise the head of his stick higher than his shoulder, on pain of the same penalty.

Rule 6: The ball may be stopped with the stick, or with any part of the person, provided that the intervening players is on his own side.

Rule 7: If the ball is kicked or thrown through the goal, or if struck beyond the goal-lines, it is to be fetched by the junior player of the side who struck the last blow, and gently thrown towards the centre peg.

Rule 8: Any player willfilly striking another, except when inflicting the penalty contained in rules 3, 4, and 5 is immediately to be excluded from the game.

The Hockey Association code prohibited the shinning penalty, and did not require players to hit from right to left, but the relationship between the codes is clear. These boy's rules, or another closely-related set of rules, developed into the Teddington rules, which in turn developed into the Hockey Association code.

While the Hockey Association rules grew in popularity, the Blackheath code did not simply disappear. In fact this club was one of the founders of the National Hockey Union in 1887, which Miroy notes was created "...with the object of playing and extending the Blackheath game, under rules similar to those of the Blackheath Hockey Club." However, the Union and the "Union Rules" ultimately did not last long; by 1895 Blackheath hockey was finished, overtaken in popularity by the Hockey Association version of the game.

Miroy posited a reason that the Association rules eventually came to be widely accepted, while the Union rules faded away. He notes that the Association use of a cricket ball, rather than the Union's rubber cube, allowed much more scientific play, and saw the development of passing and stickhandling becoming prime elements of the game rather than long passes with the ball spending a great deal of time in the air, and back-and-forth rushes.

This bears a remarkable similarity to the rise of organized hockey in Canada. When the game switched from a hard ball bouncing on the ice, to a flat disc sliding on it, the science of the game increased dramatically, as did its popularity. The phenomenon is persistent.

Comparison of Hockey Association and Montreal Rules

Hockey Association	Montreal Rules
1. Dimensions of playing area.	None, similar rule added 1893.
2. Restriction on sticks.	None, similar rule added 1886.
3. Begin play with bully, change goals at half.	1. Begin play with bully, change goals each game.
4. Procedure if ball out behind goal.	4. Procedure if ball out behind goal.
5. Procedure if ball out on side.	5. Procedure if ball out on side.
6. Offside rule, exception if three defenders in between.	2. Offside rule, no exception.
7. Stop ball but not play with body, must play from right to left, list of illegal actions.	3. Stop ball but not play with body, list of illegal actions.
8. What constitutes a goal.	None, similar rule added 1886.
9. Maximum distance a goal can be scored from.	No equivalent, ever.
10.Players must be behind ball on bully.	Part of rule 2, players must always be behind ball.
11.Infringement results in bully.	6. Infringement results in bully.
12.Eleven players per side.	None, similar rule added 1886.
No equivalent.	7. Disputes settles by umpired, referee breaks ties.

As we see from the above comparison, there is only one of the original Montreal Rules that does not derive directly from the Hockey Association code in some way. That is Rule 7, which states that all disputes are to be decided by the umpires, with a disagreement between the umpires to be finally settled by the referee. There is no reference at all to umpires or a referee in the Hockey Association rules. To complete the story of the original Montreal Rules, we need to determine where this rule came from. Was this an innovation of Creighton *et al*, or did they have some other source?

One thing we have not considered as a potential source of inspiration for the first rules of organized hockey is Canada's other national game, lacrosse. Organized lacrosse predates organized hockey by at least 10 years. The rules of the National Lacrosse Association date from 1867, when William George Beers, founder of the Montreal Lacrosse Club, wrote a code of standardized rules for the organized game. Mr. Beers was not shy about spelling things out in a goodly amount of detail, as we can see below.

Rules of Lacrosse - 1869
Source: Beers, W. G. (1869). Lacrosse, the National Game of Canada. Montreal: Dawson Brothers.

Rule 1.1 (The Crosse): The Crosse may be of any length to suit the player; woven with cat-gut, which must not be bagged. ("Cat-gut" is intended to mean raw hide, gut or clock strings, not cord or soft leather.) The netting must be flat when the ball is not on it. In its widest part the crosse shall not exceed one foot. No string must be brought through any hole at the side of the tip of the turn. A leading string, resting upon the top of the stick, may be used, but must not be fastened, so as to form a pocket, lower down the stick than to the end of the length strings. The length strings must be woven to within two inches of their termination, so that the ball cannot catch in the meshes.

Rule 1.2: Players may change their crosse during a match.

Rule 2 (The Ball): The Ball must be India rubber sponge, not less than eight and not more than nine inches in circumference. In matches, it must be furnished by the challenged party.

Rule 3 (The Goals): The Goals may be placed at any distance from each other, and in any position agreeable to the captains of both sides. The top of the flag-posts must be six feet above the ground, including any top ornament, and six feet apart. In matches they must be furnished by the challenged party.

Rule 4 (The Goal-Crease): There shall be a line or crease, to be called the Goal-Crease, drawn in front of each goal, six feet from the flag-poles, within which no opponent must stand unless the ball has passed cover-point.

Rule 5.1 (Umpires): There must be two umpires at each goal, one for each side, who must stand behind the flags when the ball is near or nearing the goal. Unless otherwise agreed upon by the captains, they must not be members of either club engaged in a match; nor shall they be changed during a match except for reasons of illness or injury. They must be thoroughly acquainted with the game, and in every way competent to act. Before a match begins, they shall draw the players up in line, and see that the regulations respecting the crosse, spiked soles, &c., are complied with. They must also see that the regulations are adhered to respecting the ball, goal, goal-crease, &c., and, in deciding any of these points, shall take the opinion of the captains and the referee. They must know, before the commencement of a match, the number of games to be played. They shall have power to decide all disputes, subject to [Rule 6], and to suspend, for any time during the match, any player infringing these laws; the game to go on during such suspension.

Rule 5.2: No umpire shall, either directly or indirectly, be interested in any bet upon the result of the match. No person shall be allowed to speak to the umpires, or in any way distract their attention, when the ball is near or nearing their goal.

Rule 5.3: When "foul" has been called, the umpires must leave their posts and cry "time," and from that time the ball must not be touched by either party, not must the players move from the positions in which they happen to be at the moment, until the umpires have returned to their posts, and "play" is called. If a player should be in possession of the ball when the umpires leave their posts, he must drop it on the ground in front. If the ball enters the goal after the umpires have left their posts, it will not count. The jurisdiction of umpires shall not extent beyond the day of their appointment. They shall not decide in any manner involving the continuance of a match beyond the day on which it is played.

31

A McGill hockey match, c.1902.

Rule 6 (Referee): The umpires shall select a referee, to whom all disputed

games and points, whereon they are a tie, may be left for decision, and who must be thoroughly acquainted with the game, and in every way competent to act. He shall take the evidence of the players particularly interested, the respective opinions of the differing umpires, and, if necessary, the opinions and offers of the captains, in cases where the discontinuance of the game is threatened. His decision shall be final. Any side rejecting his decision, by refusing to continue a match, shall be declared the losers. The referee must be on the ground at the commencement of and during the match, but during play he shall not be between the two goals.

Rule 7 (Captains): Captains, to superintend the play, may be appointed by each side, previous to the commencement of a match. They shall be members of the club by whom they are appointed, and of no other. They may or may not be players in a match: if not, they shall not carry a crosse, nor shall they be dressed in Lacrosse uniform. They shall select umpires, and toss up for choice of goal. They shall report any infringement of the laws during a match to the nearest umpires.

Rule 8 (Name of Players): The players of each side shall be designated as follows: "Goal-keeper," who defends the goal; "Point," first man out from goal; "Cover-point," in front of Point; "Centre," who faces; "Home;" nearest opponent's goal. Others shall be termed "Fielders."

Rule 9.1 (Miscellaneous): Twelve players shall constitute a full field, and they must have been regular members of the club they represent, and no other, for at least thirty days prior to a match.

Rule 9.2: A match shall be decided by the winning of three games out of five, unless otherwise agreed upon.

Rule 9.3: Captains shall arrange, previous to a match, whether it is to be played out in one day, postponed at a stated hour, or in the event of rain, darkness, &c., or to be considered a draw under certain circumstances; and, it postponed, if it is to be resumed where left off.

Rule 9.4: If postponed and resumed where left off, there shall be no change of players on either side.

Rule 9.5: Either side may claim at least five minutes' rest, and not more than ten, between each game.

Rule 9.6: No Indian must play in a match for a white club, unless previously agreed upon. [We could give the benefit of the doubt here and suggest that natives were barred from playing with whites because they were so much better at the game than white players, so it would be unfair to let them play. But I think we all know the real purpose of this rule.]

Rule 9.7: After each game, the player must change sides.

Rule 9.8: No change of players must be made after a match has commenced, except for reasons of accident of injury during a match. When a match has been agreed upon, and one side is deficient in the numbers of players, their opponents may either limit their own numbers to equalize the sides, or compel the other side to fill up the compliment.

Rule 10 (Spiked Soles): No player must wear spiked soles.

Rule 11 (Touching the Ball with the Hand): The ball must not be touched with the hand, save in case of [Rule 12] and [Rule 13].

Rule 12 (Goal-Keeper): Goal-keeper, while defending goal within the goal-crease may pat away with his hand or block the ball in any manner.

Rule 13 (Ball in Inaccessible Place): Should the ball lodge in any place inaccessible to the crosse, it may be taken out by the hand; and the part picking it up, must "face" with his nearest opponent.

Rule 14 (Ball Out of Bounds): Balls thrown out of bounds must be picked up with the hand, and "faced" for at the nearest spot within the bounds.

Rule 15 (Throwing the Crosse): No player shall throw his crosse at a player or at the ball under any circumstances.

Rule 16 (Accidental Game): Should the ball be accidentally put through a goal by one of the players defending it, it is game for the side attacking that goal. Should it be put through a goal by any one not actually a player, it shall not count.

Rule 17 (Balls Catching in the Netting): Should the ball catch in the netting, the crosse must immediately be struck on the ground as to dislodge it.

Rule 18 (Rough Play, &c.): No player shall hold another with the crosse, nor shall he grasp an opponent's stick with his hands, under his arms, or between his legs; nor shall any player hold his opponent's crosse with his crosse in any way to keep him from the ball until another player reaches it. No player shall deliberately strike or trip another, nor push with the hand; nor must any player jump at to shoulder an opponent, nor wrestle with the legs entwined so as to throw his opponent.

Rule 19 (Threatening to Strike): Any player raising his fist to strike another, shall be immediately ruled out of the match.

34

Rule 20.1 (Foul Play): Any player considering himself purposely injured during play, must report to his captain, who must report to the umpires, who shall warn the player complained of.

Rule 20.2: In the event of persistent fouling, after cautioning by the umpires, the latter may declare the match lost by the side thus offending, or may remove the offending player or players, and compel the side to finish the match short-handed.

Rule 21 (Interrupted Matches): In the event of a match being interrupted by darkness or to any other cause considered right by the umpires, and one side having won two games – the other none – the side having won the two games shall be declared winners of the match. Should one side have won two games, and the other one, the match shall be considered drawn.

Rule 22 (Amendments): Any amendment of alteration proposed to be made in any part of these laws, shall be made only at the Annual Conventions of the National Association, and by a three-fourths vote of the members present.

In Rule 5 and Rule 6, we see that in this lacrosse code the umpires are responsible for enforcing the rules of the game, with the referee present essentially to break ties between the umpires in case of a disagreement between them. These are precisely the same roles assigned to the officials in the 1877 Montreal Rules, although it did not take long before a trend began of the referee having greatly increased responsibility, and the umpires greatly decreased responsibility. We will see this trend when we examine how the rules evolved, in Appendix I.

There are a few other points in this expansive code that may have influenced organized hockey as well. For instance, while the Hockey Association code states that goals should be six yards apart, the Montreal Rules do not specify this number. We know, however, as it was later codified, that organized hockey used a standard of six feet across, which is still in use today. It may not be a coincidence that organized lacrosse goals were six feet apart as well.

Lacrosse used a face, rather than a bully, to put the ball in play. The Montreal Rules used a bully, however when the OHA developed their own code of rules in 1891, they decided upon a face instead. This was eventually adopted into the Montreal Rules as well.

The names of most of the positions in early organized hockey were drawn directly from the terms used by lacrosse in Rule 8 above: goal-keeper, point, cover-point and centre. These terms weren't universally used in the early days in hockey. The four forwards were generally just referred to as forwards, without specifying their position in more detail, until the mid-1890s. In the first few years of organized hockey in Manitoba, the point was called a back, and the cover-point and rover were called half-backs (using football terminology rather than lacrosse). Eventually the terms used in the Montreal game became the standard.

The Hockey Association code states that the teams are to change ends only at half-time, whereas the 1877 Montreal Rules require changing ends after each game (goal) is scored. Rule 9.7 of the laws of lacrosse above provide this very rule. Rule 9.8 also allows no change of players, which was not codified in the first version Montreal Rules (being introduced in 1886), but was the practice from the first days of organized hockey. Lacrosse was certainly not alone in not allowing substitutes in sports of the nineteenth century, however, so attributing this specific rule to lacrosse may be a stretch. Rules 19 and 20.2 gave the officials the ability to send players off the lacrosse field for persistent rules violations. The first Montreal Rules did not allow this; however it was added to the first revision of the rules in 1886. This could be seen as another influence of the lacrosse laws.

Taking all of this information together, then, it can be said with a good deal of certainty that the earliest rules of organized hockey were derived directly from the laws of English field hockey, but with a light sprinkling of the lacrosse code as well. This synthesis of rules, and the innovation of the puck, gave organized hockey the unique character that allowed its popularity to ultimately soar to its present levels.

Chapter Five

FOOTBALL CONNECTIONS

The line of derivation of the Montreal Rules does not truly end (or rather, begin) at the rules of English field hockey. The field hockey rules themselves were influenced by the rules of football, the earliest known code of which preceded the earliest known field hockey rules by 13 years (1848 versus 1861). The first football association (called, of course, the Football Association) also predated the Hockey Association (the Brits certainly have succinct organization naming down pat) by 12 years (1863 versus 1875).

The association football rules did not contribute a large number of rules to the Hockey Association code; really there are only two. First, the procedure for putting the ball back in play after it goes out on the side is quite similar; there is no bully as in the Eton rules. This is a fairly innocuous rule, however, and indeed the Montreal Rules would ultimately go to the Eton way in later years. But by far the most important contribution of the football code is the offside rule.

We have previously discussed that the offside rule is perhaps the single most game-defining law of early organized hockey. By 1875 the Football Association had revised its offside rule to allow an exception when there are a certain number of defenders between the attacker and the ball, which was also incorporated into the Hockey Association rules. Ironically the Montreal Rules ultimately used the older version of the offside rule from 1863, not allowing any exception to its application.

So while the Eton hockey rules provide a great deal of the basis of the eventual Hockey Association rules, it's the Football Association code that contributed the single most important rule of them all.

As we can see below, of the 1863 Association Football code, only Rules 4, 5, 6 and 10 have any relevance to the Hockey Association laws, with Rule 4 being the simple definition of a goal, and Rule 5 and Rule 10 being substantially modified. The offside rule is the only one that passes to field hockey untouched.

Association Football Rules - 1863
Source: http://en.wikipedia.org/wiki/Laws_of_the_Game
_(association_football)
Retrieved 12 Nov 2013

Rule 1: The maximum length of the ground shall be 200 yards, the maximum breadth shall be 100 yards, the length and breadth shall be marked off with flags; and the goal shall be defined by two upright posts, eight yards apart, without any tape or bar across them.

Rule 2: A toss for goals shall take place, and the game shall be commenced by a place kick from the centre of the ground by the side losing the toss for goals; the other side shall not approach within 10 yards of the ball until it is kicked off.

Rule 3: After a goal is won, the losing side shall be entitled to kick off, and the two sides shall change goals after each goal is won.

Rule 4: A goal shall be won when the ball passes between the goal-posts or over the space between the goal-posts (at whatever height), not being thrown, knocked on, or carried.

Rule 5: When the ball is in touch, the first player who touches it shall throw it from the point on the boundary line where it left the ground in a direction at right angles with the boundary line, and the ball shall not be in play until it has touched the ground.

Rule 6: When a player has kicked the ball, any one of the same side who is nearer to the opponent's goal line is out of play, and may not touch the ball himself, nor in any way whatever prevent any other player from doing so, until he is in play; but no player is out of play when the ball is kicked off from behind the goal line.

Rule 7: In case the ball goes behind the goal line, if a player on the side to whom the goal belongs first touches the ball, one of his side shall be entitled to a free kick from the goal line at the point opposite the place where the ball shall be touched. If a player of the opposite side first touches the ball, one of his side shall be entitled to a free kick at the goal only from a point 15 yards outside the goal line, opposite the place where the ball is touched, the opposing side standing within their goal line until he has had his kick.

Rule 8: If a player makes a fair catch, he shall be entitled to a free kick, providing he claims it by making a mark with his heel at once; and in order to take such kick he may go back as far as he pleases, and no player on the opposite side shall advance beyond his mark until he has kicked.

Rule 9: No player shall run with the ball.

Rule 10: Neither tripping nor hacking shall be allowed, and no player shall use his hands to hold or push his adversary.

Rule 11: A player shall not be allowed to throw the ball or pass it to another with his hands.

Rule 12: No player shall be allowed to take the ball from the ground with his hands under any pretence whatever while it is in play.

Rule 13: No player shall be allowed to wear projecting nails, iron plates, or *gutta-percha* on the soles or heels of his boots.

At the risk of entering an infinite regression of "well, then where did *those* rules come from?" we can go on to examine the origin of the Association Football code. Eventually we'll reach the point where organized sports emerged from folk games, and the trail will lead off into the mists of unwritten history. But let's go as far back as we can.

The 1863 Association Football rules were drafted by a man with the positively Dickensian moniker of Ebenezer Morley, who is now often called the father of modern football. Subsequent rule changes included reverting to an offside rule that refers to the numbers of defenders between the player and the goal in 1866, and the introduction of the specific goalkeeper position in 1871.

The Association Football code was heavily influenced by two existing sets of rules: the Cambridge rules (originating in 1848), and the more widely-used Sheffield rules (from 1858). Morley drew aspects of the Football Association rules from both of these.

The original Cambridge rules were revised by a committee in 1863, not long before the FA code was developed. These revised rules were:

Cambridge Football Rules - 1863
Source: http://en.wikipedia.org/wiki/Cambridge_rules.
Retrieved 12 Nov 2013

Rule 1: The length of the ground shall not be more than 150 yds. and the breadth not more than 100 yds. The ground shall be marked out by posts and two posts shall be placed on each side-line at distances of 25 yds. from each goal line.

Rule 2: The GOALS shall consist of two upright poles at a distance of 15 ft. from each other.

Rule 3: The choice of goals and kick-off shall be determined by tossing and the ball shall be kicked off from the middle of the ground.

Rule 4: In a match when half the time agreed upon has elapsed, the side shall change goals when the ball is next out of play. After such change or a goal obtained, the kick off shall be from the middle of the ground in the same direction as before. The time during which the game shall last and the numbers in each side are to be settled by the heads of the sides.

Rule 5: When a player has kicked the ball any one of the same side who is nearer to the opponent's goal line is OUT OF PLAY and may not touch the ball himself nor in any way whatsoever prevent any other player from doing so.

Rule 6: When the ball goes out of the ground by crossing the side lines, it is out of play and shall be kicked straight into the ground again from the point where it first stopped.

Rule 7: When a player has kicked the ball beyond the opponents' goal line, whoever first touches the ball when it is on the ground with his hand, may have a FREE kick bringing the ball straight out from the goal line.

Rule 8: No player may touch the ball behind his opponents' goal line who is behind it when the ball is kicked there.

Rule 9: If the ball is touched down behind the goal line and beyond the line of the side-posts, the FREE kick shall be from the 25 yds. post.

Rule 10: When a player has a free-kick, no-one of his own side may be between him and his opponents' goal line and no one of the opposing side may stand within 10 yds. of him.

Rule 11: A free kick may be taken in any manner the player may choose.

Rule 12: A goal is obtained when the ball goes out of the ground by passing between the poles or in such a manner that it would have passed between them had they been of sufficient height.

Rule 13: The ball, when in play may be stopped by any part of the body, but it may NOT be held or hit by the hands, arms or shoulders.

Rule 14: ALL charging is fair; but holding, pushing with the hands, tripping up and shinning are forbidden.

The most important rule that Morley drew from the Cambridge rules was Rule 5, the offside rule.

The Cambridge Rules did not gain wide acceptance outside of the region, and the Sheffield Rules had achieved much more widespread use by that time. They also had some influence on Morley's laws.

Sheffield Football Rules - 1859
Source: Rules, Regulations, & Laws of the Sheffield Foot-Ball Club, 1859.

Rule 1: Kick off from the middle must be a place kick.

Rule 2: Kick out must not be from more than 25 yards out of goal.

Rule 3: Fair Catch is a catch from any player, provided the Ball has not touched the ground, or has been thrown direct from touch, and entitles to a free kick.

Rule 4: Charging is fair in case of a place kick (with the exception of a kick off) as soon as the player offers to kick, but he may always draw back, unless he has actually touched the Ball with his foot.

Rule 5: Pushing with the hands is allowed, but no hacking or tripping up is fair play under any circumstances whatsoever.

Rule 6: No player may be held or pulled over.

Rule 7: If is not lawful to take the Ball off the ground (except in touch) for any purpose whatever.

Rule 8: The Ball may be pushed or hit with the hand, but holding the Ball (except in the case of a fair kick) is altogether disallowed.

Rule 9: A goal must be kicked, but not from touch, not by a free kick from a catch.

Rule 10: A Ball in touch is dead, consequently the side that touches it down must bring it to the edge of touch, and throw it straight out at least six yards from touch.

Rule 11: That each player must provide himself with a red and a dark blue flannel cap. One colour to be worn by each side during play.

From the Sheffield Rules, association football inherited the fair catch rule, and the prohibition against picking up the ball. Both Cambridge and Sheffield banned hacking and tripping, but Sheffield allowed pushing with the hands, while Cambridge did not, and Morley agreed with the latter. Most importantly, again, Sheffield included no offside rule. So while Sheffield contributed a few rules, the most important law came from Cambridge.

The Cambridge Rules were originally standardized by a committee at Cambridge University in 1848, in an attempt to bring students together and reduce confusion, as each man as a youth had learned to play a game called football in a different way. The text from the original rules has been lost, but a copy from 1856 still survives, and is most likely largely identical to the original.

Cambridge Football Rules – 1856
Source: http://en.wikipedia.org/wiki/Cambridge_rules.
Retrieved 12 Nov 2013.

Rule 1: This club shall be called the University Foot Ball Club.

Rule 2: At the commencement of the play, the ball shall be kicked off from the middle of the ground: after every goal there shall be a kick-off in the same way.

Rule 3: After a goal, the losing side shall kick off; the sides changing goals, unless a previous arrangement be made to the contrary.

Rule 4: The ball is out when it has passed the line of the flag-posts on either side of the ground, in which case it shall be thrown in straight.

Rule 5: The ball is behind when it has passed the goal on either side of it.

Rule 6: When the ball is behind it shall be brought forward at the place where it left the ground, not more than ten paces, and kicked off.

Rule 7: Goal is when the ball is kicked through the flag-posts and under the string.

Rule 8: When a player catches the ball directly from the foot, he may kick it as he can without running with it. In no other case may the ball be touched with the hands, except to stop it.

Rule 9: If the ball has passed a player, and has come from the direction of his own goal, he may not touch it till the other side have kicked it, unless there are more than three of the other side before him. No player is allowed to loiter between the ball and the adversaries' goal.

Rule 10: In no case is holding a player, pushing with the hands, or tripping up allowed. Any player may prevent another from getting to the ball by any means consistent with the above rules.

Rule 11: Every match shall be decided by a majority of goals.

It's here that the direct line of organized codes ends, from the rules that developed into organized hockey, all the way back to the first written set of football laws in England. Recorded history does not offer any further evidence of distinctly relevant codified rules to examine, so our search ends here.

Chapter Six

AUTHORSHIP OF THE MONTREAL RULES

There is one final issue to be discussed with respect to the first written rules of organized hockey. We have previously discussed the key role James Creighton played in the organization of the game, though so far as we know he did not claim any special importance to the game for himself during his lifetime. Although Creighton made no known claims personally, several claims have been made in the past as to the authorship of these rules.

There is no shortage of Creighton's fellow late-1870s McGill students who claimed authorship of the rules. Two of these were Richard Smith and William "Chick" Murray, both of whom played with the 1883 McGill side that won the first Montreal Winter Carnival hockey tournament. These men related stories about the early years of organized hockey, many years after the fact. Their reports contain a number of inconsistencies and errors, which is to be expected from decades-old memories. These inconsistencies and errors, I submit, are sufficient to disregard the claims, especially in light of the information presented in this book as to the origin of organized hockey rules. We will discuss their claims momentarily.

William Fleet Robertson is another McGiller who later made claims about the origin of these rules. His statements seem more believable than Smith and Murray's in some sense, but still suffer from a critical problem of inconsistencies.

Michel Vigneault, in his 2001 doctoral dissertation, discusses all three of these claims in some detail, and Earl Zuckerman references them as well in a 2000 article. I build upon these discussions here.

Smith's report was written in the January 18, 1908 edition of the *Montreal Daily Star*. He claimed that he and two other students drafted the rules of the game in September 1878, and that they were then submitted to a group of students the following September. Smith suggests that he took some rules from field hockey, designed a few of his own, and also used some rugby football rules.

One problem with Smith's story is, of course, the date. The first organized hockey match was played in March of 1875, so his suggested date is about five years too late. Creighton and his chums had been playing organized hockey for several years before Smith claims to have invented the rules. He also claimed that the first hockey game was played in December 1879, which we know to be untrue as well.

Then there is the issue of the rules themselves. We know what the earliest recorded rules of organized hockey look like. To say that these rules borrowed something from field hockey is an understatement. We have seen how these first rules were largely an edited version of the Hockey Association rules. There is little in the first rules that could be said to have been invented rather than borrowed from another sport, be it field hockey or lacrosse. The one item not directly borrowed from another code is the requirement for players to always be on their side of the ball, but even this was not unique as the 1862 Boy's Hockey Rules we examined earlier contained such a provision. This could also be seen as an influence of rugby, at least to modern eyes and indeed Smith does claim rugby influenced "his" rules. But in fact, as we'll see in Appendix II, the rules of rugby in the 1870s had no requirement for players to always be on their own side of the ball. The rules actually stated that all players were onside unless they took certain actions, and one of these actions was not simply being on the wrong side of the ball.

Smith's dates and characterizations of the rules of early organized hockey both cast doubt on the accuracy of his recollections. There is ample reason to be skeptical of them, and there is no reason to accept these claims over the records of rules and matches that we have, which were written at the time, rather than 30 years later as in the case of Smith's claims.

Smith's claims are likely the source of the idea that early organized hockey rules were influenced by rugby, since he specifically refers to that sport in his story. This, in turn, has likely led to the idea that early organized hockey's offside rules were akin to rugby, and thus many modern authors report that passes were strictly lateral in nature. As we'll see in the discussion of offside rules in Appendix I, this is not the case. And since this idea is based on an non-creditable report, it should not be surprising that it is incorrect. Smith cannot be taken at his word.

Robertson's claims come from an undated letter of his, referred to in Vigneault (2001). He claims that he witnessed a match of field hockey in England, and upon his return to McGill used his experience with that game to help organize the game there. This does have a degree of plausibility to it; after all, we know that the first organized hockey rules were based on field hockey. But again, the dates don't make sense. Robertson returned from his England trip on November 9, 1879, which would put his input into the organized hockey rules around the same time as Smith's claim, which we know to be several years too late.

Vigneault (2001) and Zuckerman (2006) both also reference Murray's claims, which were reported in a 1936 edition of the *McGill News*, nearly 60 years after the events to which they purport to relate. The problems with relying on memories so old should be apparent, especially when we compare them to historical records.

Murray's claim does have the advantage of reconciling Smith's and Robertson's claims with each other, all the while inserting himself as the original creator of the rules. Given that these claims were made many years after Smith and Robertson had made theirs, they should be expected to be consistent with the earlier claims. This means, of course, that Murray's claims have precisely the same problems as the earlier ones. Internally consistent does not mean true.

Murray claims to have himself drafted the first rules of organized hockey on November 10, 1879, over four-and-a-half years after the first match of organized hockey was actually played. He then claims to have discussed the rules with Smith the following day, and that these two, plus Robertson, revised the rules on November 12, 1879 and decided that Smith should write them down. These claims, while internally consistent, are untenable given the historical evidence we have of when organized hockey began.

Murray's claim states that the rules did not allow the stick to be lifted higher than the knee, which was the rule in some versions of field hockey. Then Smith was supposed to have revised this, making the hips the limit. We know, however, that from the first published set of organized hockey rules, the limit has always been the shoulder, a rule which was inherited from the Hockey Association code.

Smith and Robertson were both football players at McGill, and therefore Murray claims to have inserted football's offside rule into organized hockey. In this case, at least, they have the rule remembered correctly. The offside rule in early organized hockey, as we have seen in previous chapters, was inherited from association football via association hockey. However, the problems with the dates in these reports, and the other inconsistencies, overwhelm this one point to suggest that none of them can be taken at face value.

In the October 28, 1946 edition of the *Hollywood Citizen-News*, William Murray, who had lived in the United States for many decades at that point, expanded upon his story as told to reporter Jim Healy. In this article, Murray claimed that William Robertson was an Englishman who came to Montreal to introduce the English game of field hockey to Canada. Robertson was, in fact, a native of Montreal. Murray then claimed that he had the idea of moving the game to the ice since the fields in Montreal were frozen by November, and that it was his idea to cut the ball down into a puck. He also claimed to have played from 1879 to 1884 in the first hockey league, involving six clubs from Montreal. There was no ice hockey league until 1886, of course, and there were never six Montreal teams involved in such a league at once.

Almost nothing Murray relates is corroborated by historical evidence. All of these errors and inconsistencies lead me to reject his story, as well those of Smith and Robertson. There is simply no evidence to support them.

There is no better candidate for the authorship of the original rules of organized hockey than James Creighton. He is known to be an organizer of the first hockey matches, and remained involved in these matches for several years. Richard Smith and William Murray did not play in any recorded hockey matches until 1882, which further diminishes their claims. The first published set of hockey rules was in the *Montreal Gazette* in 1877, and as Zuckerman (2006) notes, Creighton was known to be a writer for that paper around that time. We do not know for certain who wrote these rules, but Vigneault concludes that Smith, Robertson and Murray did not, while Creighton is by far the most likely candidate for the honour. I am inclined to agree.

Appendix I

ANNOTATED CODES OF EARLY HOCKEY LAWS

The rules of organized hockey did not remain static, of course, fixated on the 1877 version of the Montreal Rules. Many additions and revisions were made to the rules over time, and other codes were developed by other leagues for their own use. This expansive appendix is made up of rule-by-rule commentary for a number of different codes from a number of different leagues and seasons. In this way we can examine how the laws of organized hockey evolved over time, and the differences between the most common codes in use in these years.

These codes should not be taken as the complete history of hockey rules for the leagues and years in question. There are undoubtedly some revisions missing, so when a particular rule changed may not be accurate. This is not intended to be rigorously complete (though I have included as many full codes from this era that I could get my hands on), but it is interesting and informative. We won't go any further than 1915, when the main eastern hockey league began revising its offside rule to match that of the PCHA, beginning the road to the modern offside laws.

Montreal Rules

We begin with the first printed rules of organized hockey, the 1877 Montreal Rules, which were most likely composed in 1875.

1877 MONTREAL RULES

Rule 1: The game shall be commenced and renewed by a Bully in the centre of the ground. Goals shall be changed after each game.

A "bully" was not actually defined in any code until the 1891 OHA rules, by which time it was more generally called a "face", which was eventually adopted into the Montreal Rules. A bully may not have been the same thing as a face. In a face the puck is placed by the referee between the two players, and then the referee calls "play" at which point the players go for the puck. A bully may not have involved the referee, with the players tapping their sticks together before going for the puck.

Rule 2: When a player hits the ball, any one of the same side who at such moment of hitting is nearer to the opponents' goal line is out of play, and may not touch the ball himself, or in any way whatever prevent any other player from doing so, until the ball has been played. A player must always be on his own side of the ball.

As we have seen, this is perhaps the single most game-defining rule of them all: the offside rule. It's also one of the most misunderstood, both by fans at the time, and by hockey historians today.

If you've read modern tales of how early organized hockey was played, you've probably seen it described as being made up of rushes and lateral (and backward) passes. The latter point is based on the idea that there was no "forward" passing. But this point is often misunderstood to mean that the puck cannot travel forward in any way when it is passed, which is not, in fact, what forward passing must mean in this context. Indeed, the rules themselves make no mention of the direction of travel of the puck, instead using the relative position of the players at the time the pass is made to make the offside/onside determination.

This rule refers to the positioning of players at the time the puck is struck. So when a player passes the puck to another, his teammates are onside so long as they were behind the puck when the pass was made and remain so throughout the puck's travels. The position of the pass recipient, when he receives the puck, is irrelevant. The implications of this should be obvious. But let us refer to an authority on the subject: Hall-of-Famer Art Farrell, one of the great Montreal Shamrocks forwards from the turn of the century. In 1899, Farrell described the principles of sound combination (ie, passing) play. To wit:

"A scientific player rushing down the ice with a partner will give the puck to the latter, **not in a direct line with him**, unless they are very close together, **but to a point somewhat in advance**, so that he will have to skate up to get it. The advantage in this style of passing is that the man who is to receive the rubber will not have to wait for it, but may skate on at the same rate of speed at which he was going before the puck was crossed, and proceed in his course without loss of time." *(Farrell p. 67, emphasis added)*

"When two 'wing' men play combination together, in an attack, **the puck should scarcely ever be passed directly to each other, but should be aimed** at the cushioned side of the rink, **some distance in advance of the man**, so that he may secure it on the rebound." *(Farrell p. 68, emphasis added)*

These passages make it clear that ideally, the puck had a forward trajectory when passed. The "forward" in "no forward passing" (if we must use that term here despite its anachronism) refers to the starting position of the player to be receiving the puck, not to the movement of the puck itself. According to Art Farrell, star hockey player c.1900, the best passes had the puck moving forward (that is, towards the opponent's goal), not laterally. The game was not strictly a lateral one as is rugby, it was focused on keeping the action moving forward at the speed of the players.

Although these passages were written in 1899, the offside rule used by Farrell's league at that time was exactly the same as the 1877 Montreal Rules version, except for four letters, P-U-C-K having replaced B-A-L-L in 1886. Some other rules had undergone many revisions in the intervening two decades, but the offside rule was left completely untouched.

If you're having difficulty imagining how the game worked with this offside rule, fret not. There remains a remnant of this rule in the modern game with which we're all familiar. At the moment that a puck carrier is just about to cross his opponent's blueline with the puck, this ancient offside rule is essentially in play. His teammates cannot be ahead of him, or else they'll be offside. The puck carrier can skate on with the disc, can pass it backwards or laterally (but backwards is not optimal, since he'll have to immediate stop himself), or he can make a lead pass so long as the pass recipient does not jump the gun and cross the line before the puck. He can even dump it ahead, and his teammates will be onside so long as they are not ahead of the puck when it's shot in. With the early offside rules, the puck carrier had to play as if he were perpetually just about to cross the opponent's blue line.

Another interesting implication of this rule is how important it made rebound control by goalkeepers. Under this original offside rule, a puck that strikes a goaltender and bounces back out cannot be played by a defensive player, except if that player was behind the goaltender at the time of the rebound. An exception to account for this was introduced in 1907, but until that time, all offensive players were able to touch the puck on a rebound, but likely only the goaltender on the defensive side would be onside. As such, ideally the goalkeeper would strike the puck into a corner after making a stop, and if he did not, it was dangerous indeed.

Rule 3: The ball may be stopped, but not carried or knocked on by any part of the body. No player shall raise his stick above his shoulder. Charging from behind, tripping, collaring, kicking or shinning shall not be allowed.

This type of rule should be very familiar to modern hockey fans. The puck can still be stopped by any body part, and still cannot be carried. It can now be "knocked on" (moved forward) by anything other than the hand. High-sticking, charging, tripping, kicking and slashing (shinning) are all still in the rulebook, and collaring (grabbing someone by the shirt) would be called holding today.

Rule 4: When the ball is hit behind the goal line by the attacking side, it shall be brought out straight 15 yards, and started again by a Bully; but, if hit behind by any one of the side whose goal line it is, a player of the opposite side shall hit it out from within one yard of the nearest corner, no player of the attacking side at that time shall be within 20 yards of the goal line, and the defenders, with the exception of the goal-keeper, must be behind their goal line.

These rules are inherited from field hockey, and specify where a bully (faceoff) is to take place in certain situations. This is similar to today, where the location of a faceoff is determined by the rulebook. However, unlike modern rules, in some situations the puck is put back in play with a free hit rather than a faceoff. Note also that this refers to a situation where the puck goes behind the goal line, meaning that there was no such thing as play behind the net at this time.

Rule 5: When the ball goes off at the side, a player of the opposite side to that which hit it out shall roll it out from the point on the boundary line at which it went off at right angles with the boundary line, and it shall not be in play until it has touched the ice, and the player rolling it in shall not play it until it has been played by another player, every player being then behind the ball.

When the ball (puck) went out of play, which was certainly easier at the time when the boards along the rink were only a few inches high, play was only restarted with a bully if it went off at an end. Here, we see that if it goes off at the side, it is simply put back into play by the team that did not hit it out.

Rule 6: On the infringement of any of the above rules, the ball shall be brought back and a Bully shall take place.

The noteworthy fact here is that there were no penalties as we now know them. When a rule was broken, the play stopped and a faceoff occurred. The only thing the offending team lost out on is whatever advantageous position they might have had at the time of the offence.

Rule 7: All disputes shall be settled by the Umpires, or in the event of their disagreement, by the Referee.

In the earliest days of organized hockey, the umpires (what we would now call goal judges) had more authority than the referee. Over time, the referee took on more and more responsibility, while the umpires lost much of theirs. We will see this as the rules evolve.

1886 MONTREAL RULES

Up to and including 1885, organized hockey had been limited to individual challenge matches between clubs, and brief (usually single-elimination) tournaments at the annual Montreal Winter Carnival starting in 1883. Due to a smallpox epidemic in Montreal, there would be no carnival in 1886.

So, that year four local hockey clubs made plans for a more extensive tournament to be played amongst themselves over the course of the winter. In advance of this tournament, representatives from each of the four teams met and agreed on a revised version of the Montreal Rules to be used. Unlike the relative uncertainty of the authorship of the 1877 Montreal Rules, we know that the 1886 edition was written by a committee made up of James Stewart of the Crystals (one of the best defensive defencemen of the 19th century), Jack Arnton of the Victorias (an offensively-minded defenceman), J. Swabey of McGill and J.W. Wood of the Montreal AAA.

This is the first known written revision to the 1877 Montreal Rules.

Source: Montreal Gazette, 08 Jan 1886.

Rule 1: Hockey sticks may be of any length to suit the player, but must not be more than three inches wide at any point.

This new rule, the first that puts restrictions on a player's equipment, is presumably intended primarily for goaltenders. I can't see any other player desiring to have a stick more than three inches wide anywhere but the blade.

Rule 2: The puck must be one inch thick and three inches in diameter, and of vulcanized rubber.

Whereas the first hockey pucks were made of wood, this new rule specifies the material and the size of the puck, both of which remain unchanged to this day. Some sources say that the rubber puck began to be used in 1881. But it was used by 1886 at the latest.

Rule 3: The top of the goals must be six feet above the ice, including any top ornament, and six feet apart.

The size of the goals is dictated for the first time here. Though the standard of six feet across remains to this day, these rules allow for slightly taller goals than we are used to (four feet), which will become the standard in the next rules revision in December 1886.

Rule 4: The referee and umpires shall be selected by the captains. Referee shall have power to settle all disputes on the ice, and his decision shall be final. One umpire shall be stationed at each goal; all question as to games shall be settled by the umpires, and their decision must be final. Umpires must not change goals during a match.

This is a new rule, which most likely codified existing practice. It specifies how umpires and referees are selected for a match, but really just states that the teams have to agree on them. No procedures are in place for cases where the captains cannot agree; presumably the game simply wouldn't go ahead until agreement was reached.

This is also the first example of what we'll see is the persistently declining authority of the umpires relative to the referee, referred to in the comments for 1877 Montreal Rule 7. Previously, umpires made decisions with respect to all aspects of the game, but now they only have authority in deciding whether a goal has been scored. The referee was originally only a tie-breaker when the umpires could not agree on the resolution to a dispute. That is, he refereed disagreements between the umpires, not the players. Now the referee has authority over all disputes on the ice, save for whether a goal has been scored or not.

Rule 5: Seven players shall constitute a full team. They shall be *bona fide* members of the club they represent; no player will be allowed to play for more than one club during a season.

This new rule specifies for the first time the number of players that are to be on the ice for each team. It was not previously restricted in the rules; in the earliest days the number of players who were available to play would determine the number on each team for that match.

The first recorded Montreal game in 1875 used nine players per side, and this continued as something of an informal standard into the early 1880s, though sometimes eight or even seven would be used instead. At the first Montreal Winter Carnival of 1883, teams were set at seven (apparently because the Quebec team arrived with only seven men), and this later became enshrined in the rules.

The restriction on players playing for more than one club in a year was presumably intended to exclude ringers. Even in these days of pure, honourable amateur play, of men who played solely for the love of the game, this was apparently already enough of a problem that such a rule was needed to prevent it. It is also possible that this rule was intended to make a player who belonged to more than one athletic club make a decision as to which he will play hockey for.

Rule 6: The games shall be commenced and renewed by a bully on the centre of the rink. Goals shall be changed after each game, unless otherwise agreed.

This is 1877 Montreal Rule 1, but it allows the teams to agree to not change goals after each score, whereas this had previously been mandatory.

Rule 7: A match shall be decided by the team winning the greatest number of games during a given time, games must in all cases be won by putting the puck through the goals from the front side.

The 1877 Montreal Rules did not actually specify how to determine which team win a match. Clearly not a new rule, this was simply not written down before, presumably because any sportsman would have considered it self-evident.

Rule 8: The time of matches shall be two half hours, with ten minutes rest between. In case of a tie, play will continue until one side scores a goal.

This rule sets out how long the match is supposed to be. An hour was already standard by this time, though at times in the past 90 minutes had been played. Note that the default procedure for a tie was an unlimited period of sudden-death overtime, unless the captains had agreed otherwise beforehand.

Rule 9: When the puck goes off the ice, behind the goals, it shall be taken by the referee to five yards at right angles from the goal line and there faced. When the puck goes off the ice at the sides, it shall be taken by the referee to five yards at right angles from the boundary line and there faced.

This rule combines 1877 Montreal Rule 4 and Rule 5, and makes a significant change in that every time the puck goes out of play, it is returned to play with a face. This brings this aspect of the rules in line with what we are used to today. Also note that play behind the goals is now possible, since this rule refers to the puck going off the ice rather than simply going behine the goal line.

Rule 10: The boundary line shall be latterly the extreme edge of the ice on either side of the rink.

The 1877 Montreal Rules did not define the boundary line, although they do refer to it. This must have been as self-evident, because this definition was dropped from the next rule revision in December 1886.

Rule 11: When a player hits the puck, any one of the same side, who at such moment of hitting is nearer the opponent goal line is out of play, and may not touch the puck himself, or in any way whatever prevent any other player from doing so until it has been played, a player must always be on his own side of the puck.

The offside rule (1877 Montreal Rule 2), is unchanged, the only difference being that the references to ball have been changed to puck.

Rule 12: The puck may be stopped, but not carried or knocked on by any part of the body; no player shall raise his stick above his shoulder;

charging from behind, tripping, collaring, kicking or shinning shall not be allowed, and any player, after being twice warned by the referee, it shall become his duty to rule the player off the ice for the match.

The list of prohibited actions is unchanged from 1877 Montreal Rule 3, however the referee now has the authority to send a player off for the remainder of the match, after having warned the player twice for rules violations. It's a severe, all-or-nothing penalty.

Previously, these actions were all barred, but the only repercussion was that the game would be stopped, and a bully would take place. Presumably the referee was given real power to penalize players because teams had figured out that if the opponents had a good scoring chance, you might as well do something illegal to try to stop it, since it will only stop the play and not cost your team anything. A defensive team could only benefit from an infraction.

Rule 13: The goal-keeper must not during play, lie, kneel or sit upon the ice, but must maintain a standing position.

This is a new rule, which prevents the goaltender from going to the ice to make a save. In the days when lifting the puck off the ice was more difficult due to the construction of the sticks, a goaltender doing so was probably seen to have too much of an advantage in stopping the puck by going to the ice. Thus, the restriction that he must remain standing. It's unclear whether any goaltenders had made a habit of doing this (I've never read a game report to this effect), and it may simply be codifying existing practice.

Rule 14: On the infringement of any of the above rules, the puck shall be brought back and a bully shall take place.

This is 1877 Montreal Rule 6, unchanged.

1886 AHAC RULES

The first organized hockey league was the Amateur Hockey Association of Canada (AHAC), created in December 1886. This league adopted the 1886 Montreal Rules as its code of laws, with only very minor changes made. This it to be expected, given that it was mainly the same teams organizing the AHAC as it was that revised the Montreal Rules less than a year before.

Source: Montreal Gazette, 23 Dec 1886.

Rule 1: The captains of contesting teams shall agree upon two umpires (one to be stationed at each goal) and a referee.

This is the first part of 1886 Montreal Rule 4.

Rule 2 : All questions as to games shall be settled by the umpires and their decision shall be final.

This is the third part of 1886 Montreal Rule 4.

Rule 3: All disputes on the ice shall be settled by the referee, and his decision shall be final.

This is the second part of 1886 Montreal Rule 4.

Rule 4: The game shall be commenced and renewed by a bully in the centre of the rink. Goals, six feet wide and four feet high, which shall be changed after each game, unless otherwise agreed.

This is 1886 Montreal Rule 6, with the dimensions of the goal added, and with the height of the goals changed from six feet to four.

Rule 5: When a player hits a puck, anyone of the same side who at such moment of hitting is nearer the opponent's goal line is out of play and may not touch the puck himself, or in any way prevent any other player from doing so until the puck has been played. A player must always be on his own side of the puck.

Rule 6: The puck may be stopped, but not carried or knocked on, by any part of the body. No player shall raise his stick above his shoulder. Charging from behind, tripping, collaring, kicking or shinning, shall not be allowed, and any player after having been twice warned by the referee, it shall become his duty to rule the player off for that match.

Rule 7: When the puck gets off the ice behind the goals it shall be taken by the referee to five yards at right angles from the goal line and there faced. When the puck goes off the ice at the sides it shall be taken by the referee at five yards at right angles from the boundary line and there faced.

Rule 8: The goal keeper must not, during play, lie, kneel or sit upon the ice, but must maintain a standing position.

The four rules above are 1886 Montreal Rule 11, Rule 12, Rule 9 and Rule 13 respectively, all unchanged.

Rule 9: Hockey sticks shall not be more than three inches wide at any point.

This is 1886 Montreal Rule 1, deleting the clarification that sticks can be of any length, which of course makes no difference since it was not a restriction at all.

Rule 10: Goal shall be scored when the puck shall have passed between the goal posts and below the top and passed from in front below an imaginary line across the top of posts.

This new rule specifies how one is to determine whether a goal has been scored. This surely is just the codification of existing practice, especially since the old field hockey code the 1877 Montreal Rules were based on included such a rule with very similar wording.

The wording of this rule, and the fact that the goals were made up of two posts rather than a net, allows an interesting play to score a legal goal. An offensive player behind the goal could pass the puck to a teammate in front of the goal by passing the puck between the goal posts. The teammate could then return the puck through the posts from the front, counting a legal score.

This is not a purely theoretical tactic, either. The Montreal Herald *of February 13, 1890 reported on a game between the Montreal AAA and Montreal Dominions. Here's how the game started:*

"Immediately after the start the Montrealers [AAA] forced the puck behind their opponents' goal. McDonald sent it through the posts from behind, and [Archie] McNaughton, who was in front, sent in through, scoring the first game for the champions."

It was probably not a common occurrence, due to the significant likelihood of the puck deflecting off the goaltender, but we know that it did happen and was a legal play.

Rule 11: The puck must be made of vulcanized rubber, one inch thick all through, and three inches in diameter.

This is 1886 Montreal Rule 2, unchanged.

Rule 12: A team shall be composed of seven players who shall be *bona fide* members of the club they represent. No player shall be allowed to play on more than one team during a season except in a case of a bona fide change of residence.

This is 1886 Montreal Rule 5, with the additional provision that a change of team is allowed for a legitimate change in residence. The 1886 Montreal Rules did not need to consider this possibility, since all teams involved were in Montreal. Now, with clubs competing from Ottawa and Quebec City, such a situation must be considered.

Rule 13: Two half hours with an intermission of ten minutes between will be time allowed for matches. A match will be decided by the team winning the greatest number of games during that time. In case of a tie after playing the specified two half hours, play will continue until one side secures a game, unless otherwise agreed upon between the captains before the match.

This is 1886 Montreal Rule 7 and Rule 8 combined into one. The captains now have the option to override the unlimited sudden-death overtime that was specified by the older rule.

Rule 14: No change of players must be made after a match has commenced except for reasons of accident or injury during the game.

This rule surely just codifies existing practice. Players substitutions were quite rare in organized hockey's early days. Under some codes a substitute was not even an option, however as Rule 15 below sets out, it was in the AHAC at this time.

Rule 15: Should any player be injured during a match and compelled to leave the field his side shall have the option of putting on a spare man from the reserve to equalize the teams; in the event of any dispute between the captains as to the injured player's fitness to continue the game the matter shall at once be decided by the referee.

While a team had the option of putting on a spare man in case of injury, it's unclear what they were to do if they lacked a spare player. Perhaps they had to soldier on without him; the option of the other team dropping a player to even up was not developed until the 1893 AHAC Rules.

Rule 16: Should a game be temporarily stopped, by the infringement of any of the rules the puck shall be brought back and a bully take place.

This is 1886 Montreal Rule 14, slightly reworded.

1893 AHAC RULES

Before the 1896/97 hockey season, the AHAC revised its rules. There is nothing world-shaking in this revision, but we can see the rules becoming more refined.

It is unclear precisely when this rule revision took place. However, an article entitled "Hockey in Canada" in the January 12, 1895 of *Harper's Weekly Magazine* discusses the rules of hockey as played by the AHAC at that time. It notes that the rules in question were adopted in December of 1893. The rules discussed in this article contain several differences from the 1886 edition of the code, but match this code precisely. Therefore it seems that these rules were revised in 1893, and as such will be referred to as the 1893 AHAC Rules.

Source: Tuthill, J.A. (Ed). Spalding's Athletic Library Vol VII, No. 74. 1898 Ice Hockey and Ice Polo Guide and Playing Rules.

Rule 1 (Team): A team shall be composed of seven players, who shall be bona-fide members of the clubs they represent. No player shall be allowed to play on more than one team in the same series during a season, except in the case of bona-fide change of residence.

This is 1886 AHAC Rule 12, unchanged.

Rule 2 (Game): The game shall be commenced and renewed by a face in the centre of the rink. Rink must be at least 112 feet by 58 feet.

1886 AHAC Rule 4 provides the first part of this rule, to which the minimum rink dimensions have been added. While the dimensions of the Victoria Skating Rick (204 feet by 80 feet), where the first organized hockey matches were played, is very similar to modern NHL standards, this rule allows for a playing surface of as little as 40% of that area.

Certainly the players were smaller in those days, but there were more of them on the ice at a time. Playing on such a small surface as the minimum allowed by these rules must have been terribly cramped.

Rule 3 (Goals): Goals shall be six feet wide and four feet high.

This is from 1886 AHAC Rule 4.

Rule 4 (Face): The puck shall be faced by being placed between the sticks of two opponents, and the Referee then calling "play." The goals shall be placed at least ten feet from the edge of the ice.

This is very similar to 1891 OHA Rule 5, which is the first codification of a faceoff procedure, though it does not specify which part of the puck was supposed to be on the ice, as the OHA did.

Some sources claim that a bully, the term used in previous versions of the Montreal rules, was like a bully still used in field hockey today rather than the face described above. That is, the puck would be placed between the two players, who would then tap their sticks together before going for the puck. If this is the case, then 1893 AHAC Rule 4 is actually a rule change, and one that seems inspired by the OHA. I have not been able to confirm this, however it is eminently plausible, even likely.

Rule 5 (Match): Two half hours, with an intermission of ten minutes between, will be the time allowed for matches, but no stops of more than fifteen minutes will be allowed. A match will be decided by the team winning the greatest numbers of games during that time. In case of a tie after playing the specified two half hours, play will continue until one side secures a game, unless otherwise agreed upon between the captains before the match. Goals shall be changed after each half hour.

This is largely the same as 1886 AHAC Rule 13, with a couple of additions. First, the requirement to change goals after each score is removed, and now both teams play the same amount of time from each end. Also, there is a new 15-minute limit on stoppages. Stoppages could be a problem at times, because of the limit on player substitutions. If a player was hurt, his team could put on a sub, or they could try to wait it out to see if he recovered (or, of course, wait it out in order to get a long rest at the expense of the shivering audience). Lengthy delays are undesirable for spectator sports, and this rule is presumably intended to keep the game going in a reasonable time.

Rule 6 (Change of Players): No change of players shall be made after a match has commenced, except for reasons of accidents or injury during the game.

This is 1886 AHAC Rule 14, unchanged.

Rule 7: Should any player be injured during a match and compelled to leave the ice, his side shall have the option of putting on a spare man from the reserve to equalize the teams. However, should a player be injured during the second half, the captain of the opposing team shall have the option of dropping a man to equalize the teams or allow his opponents to put on a spare man. In the event of any dispute between the captains as to the injured player's fitness to continue the game, the matter shall at once be decided by the Referee.

This is another adaptation in order to move the match along in case of injury. Under 1886 AHAC Rule 15, an injured man could be subbed by his side; here, in the second half (where injuries were more common due to fatigue), the other side could instead drop a man to even up. This helps to prevent the other side from trying to finagle a lengthy stoppage from an apparent injury.

Rule 8 (Stoppages): Should a game be temporarily stopped by the infringement of any of the rules, the captain of the opposite team may claim that the puck be taken back and a face take place where it was last played from before such infringement occurred.

This rule builds on 1886 AHAC Rule 16, where the face could now be taken where the puck was when the play was stopped, rather than where the infringement occurred.

Per Kitchen (2000), this rule change was instituted before the 1888/89 season. It is unknown if any other changes from this code of laws were actually made before 1893.

Rule 9 (Off-Side): When a player hits the puck, any one of the same side who at such moment of hitting is nearer the opponent's goal line is out of play, and may not touch the puck himself or in any way whatever prevent any other player from doing so until the puck has been played. A player must always be on his own side of the puck.

The offside rule is straight from 1886 AHAC Rule 5, unchanged since the 1877 code. At this point in the evolution of organized hockey laws, only two original rules really remain untouched: matches begin with a faceoff (although a face may in fact be different than a bully), and offsides. The offside rule is vital to how the game is played on the ice, and it is relatively complex, so it presumably was functioning as intended, since it survived rule revision after rule revision in its original state.

Rule 10 (Knocking on, Charging, Etc.): The puck may be stopped, but not carried or knocked on, by any part of the body. No player shall raise his stick above his shoulder except in lifting the puck. Charging from behind, tripping, collaring, kicking or shinning shall not be allowed, and any player after having been warned by the Referee, he may rule the player off the ice for the game or match, or for such portion of actual playing time as he may deem fit.

Here we see the penalty rules becoming more refined. An exception is added to the high-sticking restriction in the case of a player lifting the puck, which does not simply refer to lifting the puck off the ice with a pass or a shot, but intentionally lifting the puck high into the air and down the ice, to clear it out of danger, which was a common tactic in early organized hockey, long before the icing rule.

Also noteworthy compared to 1886 AHAC Rule 6 is the fact that the referee now only has to warn a player once instead of twice before sending him off. Clearly the old rules were not doing enough to

68

discourage players from rule-breaking. But to offset the resulting greater frequency of sendoffs, the referee is given discretion as to how long the player is to be sent off for, while previously it was the match or nothing.

Rule 11 (Puck Off Ice): When the puck goes off the ice or a foul occurs behind the goals it shall be taken by the Referee to five yards at right angles from the goal line and there faced. When the puck goes off the ice at the sides it shall be taken by the Referee to five yards at right angles from the boundary line and there faced.

Rule 12 (Goal-keeper): The goal-keeper must not, during play, lie, kneel or sit upon the ice, but must maintain a standing position.

Rule 13 (Score): Goal shall be scored when the puck shall have passed between the goal posts from in front and below an imaginary line across the top of posts.

Rule 14 (Sticks): Hockey sticks shall not be more than three inches wide at any point.

Rule 15 (Puck): The puck must be made of vulcanized rubber, one inch all through and three inches in diameter.

The five rules above are 1886 AHAC Rule 7, Rule 8, Rule 10, Rule 9 and Rule 11 respectively, all unchanged.

Rule 16 (Officials): The captains of the contesting teams shall agree upon a Referee and two Umpires (one to be stationed behind each goal), which positions shall not be changed during a match, and two Timekeepers. In the event of the captains failing to agree upon Umpires and Timekeepers the Referee shall appoint same.

This expansion of 1886 AHAC Rule 1 introduces two timekeepers to the ranks of the match officials. Presumably, before this time the referee had to keep time as well, since he was in charge of everything that happened on the ice.

Rule 17 (Referee): All disputes on the ice shell be settled by the Referee, and his decision shall be final.

This is 1886 AHAC Rule 3, unchanged.

Rule 18 (Umpires): All questions as to games shall be settled by the Umpires, and their decisions shall be final. In the event of any dispute as to the decision of an Umpire the Referee shall have power to remove and replace him.

This is 1886 AHAC Rule 2, with the added authority of the Referee to remove Umpires in the event of a dispute. The erosion of the authority of the umpire, and the increase of that of the referee, continues.

1899 CAHL RULES

When the AHAC became the Canadian Amateur Hockey League (CAHL) before the 1898/99 season, some minor revisions were made to the code of play. The 1899 CAHL rules are almost identical to the 1893 version of the AHAC rules; the only significant changes have to do with the penalty rules, where additional offences are added.

Source: Farrell (1899).

Rule 1: A Team shall be composed of seven players, who shall be bona-fide members of the Clubs they represent. No player shall be allowed to play on more than one team in the same series during a season, except in the case of bona-fide change of residence.

This is 1893 AHAC Rule 1, unchanged.

Rule 2: The game shall be commenced and renewed by a face in the centre of the rink. Rink must be at least 112 feet by 58 feet. Goals shall be six feet wide and four feet high.

1893 AHAC Rule 2 and Rule 3 are merged together here.

Rule 3 (Definition of a Face): The Puck shall be faced by being placed between the sticks of two opponents, and the Referee then calling "play." The goals shall be placed at least ten feet from the edge of the ice.

Rule 4: Two half hours, with an intermission of ten minutes between, will be the time allowed for matches, but no stops of more than fifteen minutes will be allowed. A match will be decided by the team winning the greatest numbers of games during that time. In case of a tie after playing the specified two half hours, play will continue until one side secures a game, unless otherwise agreed upon between the captains before the match. Goals shall be changed after each half hour.

Rule 5: No change of players shall be made after a match has commenced, except for reasons of accidents or injury during the game.

The three rules above are 1893 AHAC Rule 4, Rule 5 and Rule 6 respectively, all unchanged.

Rule 6: Should any player be injured during a match and compelled to leave the ice, his side shall be allowed to put on a spare man from the reserve to equalize the teams; should any player be injured during the second half of the match the captain of the opposing team shall have the option of dropping a player to equalize the teams or allow his opponents to put on a man from the reserve. In the event of any dispute between the captains as to the injured player's fitness to continue the game, the matter shall at once be decided by the Referee.

This is 1893 AHAC Rule 7 with only minor rewordings that do not change its meaning.

Rule 7: Should a game be temporarily stopped by the infringement of any of the rules, the captain of the opposite team may claim that the puck be taken back and a face take place where it was last played from before such infringement occurred.

Rule 8: When a player hits the puck, any one of the same side, who at such moment of hitting is nearer the opponent's goal-line, is out of play and may not touch the puck himself, or in any way whatever prevent any other player from doing so, until the puck has been played. A player must always be on his own side of the puck.

The two rules above are 1893 AHAC Rule 8 and Rule 9 respectively, both unchanged.

Rule 9: The puck may be stopped, but not carried or knocked on, by any part of the body, nor shall any player close his hand on, or carry the puck to the ice in his hand. No player shall raise his stick above the shoulder, except in lifting the puck. Charging from behind, tripping, collaring, kicking or shinning shall not be allowed, and for any infringement of these rules, the Referee may rule the offending player off the ice for that match, or for such portion of actual playing time as he may see fit.

To 1893 AHAC Rule 10 prohibitions are added against closing the hand on puck and carrying the puck to the ice in hand. The referee is also no longer required to warn a player before sending him off, so players were presumably still pushing the envelope too much for the league's liking.

Rule 10: When the puck goes off the ice or a foul occurs behind the goals it shall be taken by the Referee to five yards at right angles from the goal line and there faced. When the puck goes off the ice at the sides it shall be taken by the Referee to five yards at right angles from the boundary line and there faced.

Rule 11: The goal-keeper must not during play, lie, kneel or sit upon the ice, but must maintain a standing position.

Rule 12: Goal shall be scored when the puck shall have passed between the goal posts from in front below an imaginary line across the top of posts.

Rule 13: Hockey sticks shall not be more than three inches wide at any part.

Rule 14: The puck must be made of vulcanized rubber, one inch all through and three inches in diameter.

Rule 15: The captains of the contesting teams shall agree upon a referee and two umpires (one to be stationed behind each goal), which positions shall not be changed during a match, and two timekeepers. In the event of the captains failing to agree on umpires and timekeepers the referee shall appoint same.

The above six rules are 1893 AHAC Rule 11 through Rule 16

respectively, all unchanged.

Rule 16: All disputes during the match shall be decided by the Referee, and he shall have full control of all players and officials from commencement to finish of matches, inclusive of stops, and his decision shall be final.

This is 1893 AHAC Rule 17, with added emphasis on the authority of the referee.

Rule 17: All questions as to games shall be settled by the Umpires, and their decisions shall be final.

1893 AHAC Rule 18 is divided into this rule and the next.

Rule 18: In the event of any dispute as to the decision of an Umpire or Time-keeper, the Referee shall have power to remove and replace him.

In addition to the referee's ability to remove an umpire, he now also has the authority to do the same to timekeepers.

Rule 19: Any player guilty of using profane or abusive language to any officials or other players shall be liable to be ruled off by the Referee, as per [Rule 9].

An additional sending-off offence is added here, interestingly not as part of Rule 9 but in its own rule. This reflects the ad hoc nature of rules updates in early organized hockey.

1904 CAHL RULES

Before the 1903/04 season, the CAHL amended its official rules. However, none of these rules deal with how the game is to be played; the modifications are all with respect to the equipment to be used, and the starting time of matches only.

Source: Farrell, Arthur (1904). Spalding's Athletic Library Ice Hockey and Ice Polo Guide. New York: American Sports Publishing Company.

Rule 1: A Team shall be composed of seven players, who shall be bona-fide members of the Clubs they represent. No player shall be allowed to play on more than one team in the same series during a season, except in the case of bona-fide change of residence.

This is 1899 CAHL Rule 1, unchanged.

Rule 2: The game shall be commenced and renewed by a face in the centre of the rink. Rink must be at least 112 feet by 58 feet. Goals shall be six feet wide and four feet high, and provided with goal nets, such as approved of by the League.

This is 1899 CAHL Rule 2, with the addition that goal nets are to be used. The 1901 AAHL Rules are the first code to mention the use of goals nets.

Rule 3 (Definition of a Face): The Puck shall be faced by being placed between the sticks of two opponents, and the Referee then calling "play." The goals shall be placed at least ten feet from the edge of the ice.

This is 1899 CAHL Rule 3, unchanged.

Rule 4: Two half hours, with an intermission of ten minutes between, will be the time allowed for matches, but no stops of more than fifteen minutes will be allowed. A match will be decided by the team winning the greatest numbers of games during that time. In case of a tie after playing the specified two half hours, play will continue until one side secures a game, unless otherwise agreed upon between the captains before the match. Goals shall be changed after each half hour.

All matches must be started at the advertised time, and if, for any reason, there be more than fifteen minutes delay in the commencement of a match the club at fault shall pay to the League as a penalty the sum of $10, unless good reason be given for such delay. The referee is to see that this rule is observed, and to notify the League within two days should any breach of it occur.

The first part of this rule is 1899 CAHL Rule 4. A fine for the late start of games has been added, in an effort to prevent unnecessary delays in getting matches underway.

Rule 5: No change of players shall be made after a match has commenced, except for reasons of accidents or injury during the game.

Rule 6: Should any player be injured during the first half of the match and compelled to leave the ice, his side shall be allowed to put on a spare man from the reserve to equalize the teams; should any player be injured during the second half of the match the captain of the opposing team shall have the option of dropping a player to equalize the teams or allow his opponents to put on a man from the reserve. In the event of any dispute between the captains as to the injured player's fitness to continue the game, the matter shall at once be decided by the referee.

Rule 7: Should a game be temporarily stopped by the infringement of any of the rules, the captain of the opposite team may claim that the puck be taken back and a face take place where it was last played from before such infringement occurred.

Rule 8: When a player hits the puck, any one of the same side, who at such moment of hitting is nearer the opponent's goal-line, is out of play and may not touch the puck himself, or in any way whatever prevent any other player from doing so, until the puck has been played. A player must always be on his own side of the puck.

Rule 9: The puck may be stopped but not carried or knocked on by any part of the body, nor shall any player close his hand on, or carry the puck to the ice in his hand. No player shall raise his stick above the shoulder, except in lifting the puck. Charging from behind, tripping, collaring, kicking or shinning shall not be allowed, and for any infringement of these rules, the Referee may rule the offending player off the ice for that match, or for such portion of actual playing time as he may see fit.

Rule 10: When the puck goes off the ice or a foul occurs behind the goals it shall be taken by the referee to five yards at right angles from the goal line and there faced. When the puck goes off the ice at the sides it shall be taken by the referee to five yards at right angles from the boundary line and there faced.

Rule 11: The goal-keeper must not during play, lie, kneel or sit upon the ice, but must maintain a standing position.

The above seven rules are 1899 CAHL Rule 5 through Rule 11 respectively, all unchanged.

Rule 12: Goal shall be scored when the puck shall have passed between the goal posts from in front below an imaginary line across the top of posts.

This rule has not changed from 1899 CAHL Rule 12, even though it should have. The reference to goal nets in Rule 2 should make the reference in this rule to an imaginary line across the top of the goal posts unnecessary.

Rule 13: Hockey sticks shall not be more than three inches wide at any part.

This is 1899 CAHL Rule 13, unchanged.

Rule 14: The puck must be made of vulcanized rubber, one inch all through and three inches in diameter.

The Spalding hockey puck, the official puck of the League, must be used in all matches. The home club to furnish the referee with a new puck previous to the match.

This is 1899 CAHL Rule 14, with the addition that only one particular brand of puck is to be used in CAHL matches. Also, it seems that typically only one puck is needed for a match, which is a rather different situation than today.

Rule 15: The captains of the contesting teams shall agree upon a referee and two umpires (one to be stationed behind each goal), which positions shall not be changed during a match, and two timekeepers. In the event of the captains failing to agree on umpires and timekeepers the referee shall appoint same.

Rule 16: All disputes during the match shall be decided by the Referee, and he shall have full control of all players and officials from commencement to finish of matches, inclusive of stops, and his decision shall be final.

Rule 17: All questions as to games shall be settled by the Umpires, and their decisions shall be final.

Rule 18: In the event of any dispute as to the decision of an Umpire or Time-keeper, the Referee shall have power to remove and replace him.

Rule 19: Any player guilty of using profane or abusive language to any officials or other players shall be liable to be ruled off by the Referee, as per [Rule 9].

The above five rules are 1899 CAHL Rule 15 through Rule 19 respectively, all unchanged.

1909 ECHA RULES

Before the 1908/09 season, the Eastern Canada Hockey Association (ECHA), successor to the CAHL, amended its code of laws. Other than the addition of an assistant referee, the changes are minor. There is evidence that some of these changes were made before the 1905/06 season, and others before the 1906/07 season, however I have not found complete codes from these seasons to confirm this. The annual Spalding guides were often remiss in ensuring they had the most up-to-date versions of the rules they printed.

Source: Toombs, Frederick R. (Ed.) (1909). Spalding's Athletic Library Office Ice Hockey Guide 1909. New York: American Sports Publishing Company.

Rule 1: A Team shall be composed of seven players, who shall be bona-fide members of the Clubs they represent. No player shall be allowed to play on more than one team in the same series during a season, except in the case of bona-fide change of residence from one city to another at least fifty miles apart.

This is 1904 CAHL Rule 1, with an additional proviso attached to the change in residence rule, that the move has to be at least 50 miles. At this time, the ECHA only had teams in Ottawa, Quebec and two in Montreal (Wanderers and Shamrocks). So, effectively a player would not be able to play for both the Wanderers and Shamrocks in the same season. But this rule is likely a holdover from before the league became fully professional this season. Such restrictions are not necessary for professional hockey.

Rule 2: The game shall be commenced and renewed by a face in the centre of the rink. The puck shall be faced by being placed between the sticks of two opponents, and the referee then calling "play." The goals shall be placed at least ten feet from the edge of the ice.

This is 1904 CAHL Rule 2 and Rule 3 combined, but the minimum rink dimensions and references to the construction of the goals have been removed.

Rule 3: Two half-hours, with an intermission of ten minutes between, will be the time allowed for matches, but no stops of more than fifteen minutes will be allowed. A match will be decided by the team winning the greatest numbers of games during that time. In case of a tie after playing the specified two half-hours, play will continue until one side secures a game, unless otherwise agreed upon between the captains before the match. Goals shall be changed after each half hour.

This is the first part of 1904 CAHL Rule 4, removing the second part that refers to the fine for a match starting late.

Rule 4: No change of players shall be made after a match has commenced, except for reasons of accident or injury during the game. *This is 1904 CAHL Rule 5, unchanged.*

Rule 5: In the event of a player being injured or compelled to leave the ice during a match, he may retire from the game for the period of ten minutes playing time, but play must be commenced immediately without the teams leaving the ice, the opposite team dropping a player to equalize. If at the expiration of ten minutes the injured player is unable to resume his position on the ice, his captain may put on a substitute, providing the injury occurred during the first half of the match. If, however, the player was injured during the second half, the opposing captain shall have the option of dropping a man for the balance of the playing time or allowing the injured player's side to put on a substitute. The man dropped to equalize shall return to the ice when the injured player does or when substitute is put on. In the event of a dispute between the captains as to the injured player's fitness to continue the game, the matter shall at once be decided by the referee, and his decision shall be final. An injured player may not resume play after his place has been filled by a substitute, without the consent of the opposing team's captain.

Much of this rule is similar to 1904 CAHL Rule 6, however the substitution rules are once again being tinkered with. No rule has seen so much finagling over the life of organized hockey as the substitution

80

rule. It seems no satisfactory law is ever arrived at. Perhaps this is a significant reason that unlimited substitutions eventually became part of the game, in order to avoid this headache.

According to Coleman (1966), the changes to this rule were made before the 1906/07 season.

Rule 6: Should the game be temporarily stopped by the infringement of any of the rules, the captain of the opposite team may claim that the puck be taken back and a face take place where it was last played from before such infringement occurred.

This is 1904 CAHL Rule 7, unchanged.

Rule 7: When a player hits the puck, any one of the same side, who at such moment of hitting is nearer the opponent's goal-line, is out of play and may not touch the puck himself, or in any way whatever prevent any other player from doing so, until the puck has been played. A player must always be on his own side of the puck. In the event of the puck rebounding off the goal keeper's body, players of his team touching the puck are to be considered on side.

Here the ECHA, like the OHA in 1905, adds an exception to its offside rule (1904 CAHL Rule 8) for rebounds off of goaltenders. This was added to the code before the 1906/07 season according to Coleman (1966).

Rule 8: The puck may be stopped but not carried or knocked on by any part of the body, nor shall any player close his hand on, or carry the puck to the ice in his hand. No player shall raise his stick above the shoulder, except in lifting the puck. Charging from behind, tripping, collaring, kicking or shinning shall not be allowed, and for any infringement of these rules, the referee or his assistant may rule the offending player off the ice for that match, or for such portion of actual playing time as he may see fit, but it shall not be necessary to stop the game to enforce this rule.

This is CAHL Rule 9, modified to apparently allow a referee to impose a penalty on a player without stopping the play. It seems the play could go on while the referee sends the offender to the side. Presumably the assistant referee would take on this task, allowing the referee to continue to monitor the continuing play.

Rule 9: When the puck goes off the ice or a foul occurs behind the goals it shall be taken by the referee to five yards at right angles from the goal line and there faced. When the puck goes off the ice at the sides it shall be taken by the referee to five yards at right angles from the boundary line and there faced.

Rule 10: The goal-keeper must not during play, lie, kneel or sit upon the ice, but must maintain a standing position.

Rule 11: Goal shall be scored when the puck shall have passed between the goal posts from in front below an imaginary line across the top of posts.

Rule 12: Hockey sticks shall not be more than three inches wide at any part.

Rule 13: The puck must be made of vulcanized rubber, one inch all through and three inches in diameter.

The Spalding hockey puck, the official puck of the League, must be used in all matches. The home club to furnish the referee with a new puck previous to the match.

The above five rules are 1904 CAHL Rule 10 through Rule 14 respectively, all unchanged.

Rule 14: The captains of the competing teams shall agree upon two timekeepers, one penalty timekeeper, two umpires (one to be stationed behind each goal, which positions shall not be changed during a match).

In the event of the captains failing to agree on umpires and timekeepers the referee shall appoint them.

This is 1904 CAHL Rule 15, with the addition of a penalty timekeeper. Also, the captains are no longer tasked with selecting a referee for the match, who is presumably now assigned by the league.

Rule 15: All disputes during the match shall be decided by the Referee, and he shall have full control of all players and officials from commencement to finish of matches, inclusive of stops, and his decision shall be final.

Rule 16: All questions as to games shall be settled by the Umpires, and their decisions shall be final.

Rule 17: In the event of any dispute as to the decision of an umpire or timekeeper, the referee shall have power to remove and replace him.

The above three rules are 1904 CAHL Rule 16 through Rule 18 respectively, all unchanged.

Rule 18: Any player guilty of using profane or abusive language to any officials or other players shall be liable to be ruled off by the referee or his assistant for the match or for such portion of actual playing time as he may see fit.

There are minor changes here to 1904 CAHL Rule 19, but none that change the effect of the rule. Strangely this rule has still not been incorporated into the general penalty rule (Rule 8), even though a violation of this rule has the same repercussions. This is the result of the ad hoc development of these rules. No systematic revision of the Montreal rules had been undertaken, unlike in the AAHL which performed a thorough, systematic rules revision before the 1908/09 season as we'll see.

Rule 19: The referee shall, previous to the commencement of the match for which he has been duly appointed or agreed upon, obtain from the captains of each of the competing clubs a full list of the players of their respective teams, and, if during the match a substitute is used by either club, the captain of the club using each substitute shall give to the referee the name of such substitute player, and same will be inclined [sic] in the list of names of said team.

The referee shall, before starting a match, see that the necessary penalty timekeeper, timekeepers and umpires have been appointed and are in their respective places. In the event of the competing clubs failing to agree upon umpires and timekeepers the referee shall appoint same. The referee shall have full control of all officials and players during the match (including stops), he shall face the puck at the commencement of each half and at such other times as may be necessary, he shall also call off-sides or rule offending players off for such period of playing time as he may see fit, and perform such other duties as may be provided for hereinafter or in the laws of hockey or championship rules.

The referee shall order the team on the ice at the advertised time, and if for any reason there be more than fifteen minutes delay in the commencement of the match, the referee shall state in his report to the Secretary of the Association the cause of this delay, and name the club or clubs if they be at fault. It will be the referee's duty to record the time of the starting and finishing of the match, as well as the games scored, mailing to the Secretary of the Association, within three days of date of match, on the forms provided for the purpose, a report of the match in detail, including the names of players penalized, together with the number and length of penalties imposed (this information to be obtained from the penalty timekeeper, who shall also keep for the referee a record of the games scored, and, if possible, who by and the time).

Should the assistant appointing or agreed upon be made to act at the last minute, or through sickness or accident be unable to finish the match, the referee shall gave power to appoint another in his stead, if he deems it necessary or if requested to do so by the captain of one of the competing teams.

This monstrosity of a rule sets out (in great detail), the responsibilities of the referee before, during and after the game. The OHA was the first code to attempt to delineate the referee's job in its code of laws, but never to this extent. It renders Rule 15 completely redundant, which is another sign that the code is in need of a thorough revision rather than the piecemeal additions and modifications that have been the norm since the game was organized.

Rule 20: The assistant referee will during the period of a match be under the control of the referee; he shall, however, have full power to stop the game should an offside or foul occur which has escaped the notice of the referee. He shall also have power to rule off for such time as he may see fit any player committing a foul. He shall also perform such other duties as may be assigned to him by the referee from time to time. If owing to illness or accident, the referee is unable to continue to officiate, the assistant shall perform such duties as devolve upon the referee during the balance of the match, selecting an assistant if he deems it necessary or if requested to do so by the captain of one of the competing teams.

Again, this is a new rule outlining the responsibilities of an official in great detail. Coleman (1966) states the second referee was added to the ECAHA rules for the 1905/06 season.

Rule 21: The penalty timekeeper shall keep a complete record of the penalties imposed by the referee or his assistant, and shall have control of all players while serving the time of their penalties, and any player ruled off shall not return to the ice until the playing time for which he was penalized has expired and then only be permission of the penalty timekeeper.

A record of the games scored, who scored by and the time of each shall be recorded by the penalty timekeeper, and this, together with a record of the penalties imposed, shall be handed the referee at the close of the match.

Finally, this is another new rule specifying the duties of a particular game official. We also find reference to official game reports, which suggests the ECHA was the first league able to produce official player statistics.

1911 NHA RULES

The National Hockey Association undertook a major revision to its code of hockey laws before the 1911/12 hockey season. Unfortunately, the best source for complete hockey rules from this period of time, the Spalding Ice Hockey Guides, were remiss in updating the professional league's rules in their publications for a number of years. As late as the 1917 edition of the Spalding guide, they were still printing the 1909 version of the rules, as evidenced by the fact the first rule still made reference to seven players making up a team, even though this was reduced to six in the 1911 rule revision.

Fortunately, the December 27, 1911 edition of the *Quebec Chronicle* printed an article detailing all of the extensive changes made to the code. Based on the structure of the 1915 code, and the fact that the author of this article seemed to be going through the code rule-by-rule, we can attempt to reconstruct the 1911 code, as follows. Although some of the below is likely the actual text of the rules, much of it certainly is not. These rules cannot be considered complete; although they have been checked against the rule changes listed in Coleman (1966).

In addition, these rules have a great deal in common with the 1911 PCHA code (as we'll see). As such, much of the text of the PCHA rules is most likely identical to what the actual text of the 1911 NHA rules, if we were to have it.

Source: Quebec Chronicle, 27 Dec 1911.

Rule 1: "In regard to composition of teams, the rule reads that at the beginning of each match clubs shall have at least nine players in uniform. Should major fouls or accident occur after all the above players have participated, the opposing club must drop one of their players to equalize. Each team shall be composed of six players who shall bear a number on their left arm."

Rule 2: "The home club shall have the privilege of choosing the goals to defend at the beginning of a game."

Rule 3: "Three periods of twenty minutes, with an intermission of ten minutes between, will be the time allowed for matches. In case of a tie, play shall continue until one side shall have scored a game, unless otherwise agreed upon before the match. Any extra period played shall be considered part of the match."

Rule 4: "Player may be changed at any time by captains, and substitutes shall be placed on the ice and original players removed without interruption, it being understood, however, that a player once removed cannot return to the ice."

Rule 5: "In the event of a player being injured he may retire for ten minutes, but play much continue without teams leaving the ice. A goal keeper will be allowed ten minutes to recuperate, however. If at the end of ten minutes a player cannot return, a substitute can be put on, the the injured player can not re-enter the game."

Rule 6: "In case of infringement of rules, the captain of the team not at fault may claim that the puck be taken back and placed where it was played from."

Rule 7: This rule most likely deals with the faceoff procedure for a puck having gone out of bounds. "The facing of the puck, rules regarding the goal-keeper, dimensions of puck and stick, scoring of goals, etc., remain as usual."

Rule 8: "The rule governing offside play remains practically as it was."

Rule 9: "Major fouls are described as any foul which physically injures or incapacitates an opposing player, throwing sticks which might prevent scoring a game, cross-checking, striking an opponent, deliberate tripping, charging from behind, collaring, kicking or hooking, striking or using foul language to an official in any player or at any time; any player penalized for a major foul shall be banished from the game and replaced by a substitute. The banished player shall carry a fine of $5 for the first offence, increasing $8 each subsequent offence until a maximum of $25 has been reached. Any fine levied must be paid by the player."

Rule 10: "Major fouls [sic, should be minor fouls] are described as kicking, holding, throwing or batting the puck, raising the stick above the shoulder except in hitting the puck and deliberate loafing offside. For violation of above a warning and then a fine of $5 is to be imposed. Any club paying the fine of its player shall be fined $200."

Rule 11: This rule most likely deals with the scoring of goals. "The facing of the puck, rules regarding the goal-keeper, dimensions of puck and stick, scoring of goals, etc., remain as usual."

Rule 12: This rule most likely deals with restrictions on the goalkeeper. "The facing of the puck, rules regarding the goal-keeper, dimensions of puck and stick, scoring of goals, etc., remain as usual."

Rule 13: This rule most likely deals with the dimensions of the stick. "The facing of the puck, rules regarding the goal-keeper, dimensions of puck and stick, scoring of goals, etc., remain as usual."

Rule 14: This rule most likely deals with the dimensions of the puck. "The facing of the puck, rules regarding the goal-keeper, dimensions of puck and stick, scoring of goals, etc., remain as usual."

Rule 15: "The president of the association shall appoint a referee, and assistance, a time keeper, penalty recorder, two umpires (one behind each goal, which position shall not be changed during a match), and will be paid such compensation as decided upon by the association."

Rule 16: "All disputes shall be decided by the referee, and his decision shall be final."

Rule 17, 18 and 19: "The duties of the referees, umpire, penalty recorder and time keepers are set forth at length."

1915 NHA RULES

In 1916, the NHA aligned its offside rule with the PCHA, which saw the beginning of forward passing being allowed in eastern hockey, in the centre ice area at first. Eventually this rule would be expanded to reach essentially modern standards by the end of the 1930 NHL season.

Since we do not have a full copy of the rules preceding this version, a point-by-point comparison is not appropriate. Comments on only a few items will suffice. This code does not constitute a comprehensive revision, but is once again a continuation of the practice of ad hoc changes.

Source: Howard, Thomas A. (Ed.) (1918). Spalding's Athletic Library Official Ice Hockey Guide 1918. New York: American Sports Publishing Co.

Rule 1 (Composition of Team): A team shall be composed of six players, who shall be bona-fide members of the clubs they represent, each player shall wear a number on the back of his sweater, numbers must be at least 10 inches, which number he shall retain while he is under contract with respective clubs.

Rule 1(a): At the beginning of each match clubs shall have at least nine players in uniform.

In the oldenest of days, teams would often not even have a single substitute player available for a match. Now, they were required to have at least three. A spare goaltender was still quite rare, however Ottawa did employ one in 1912/13 and 1913/14, as a young Clint Benedict was being groomed to replace the aging Percy LeSueur.

Rule 1(b): Should minor, major or match fouls or accidents occur after all the above number of players have participated in a match and are not available for play, either through injury or banishment, the opposing club must drop one of their players to equalize.

Rule 2: The game shall be commenced and renewed by a face in the centre of the rink.

Rule 2(a): Visiting club shall have the choice of goals to defend at the start of the game.

Rule 2(b): The puck shall be faced by the referee dropping the puck on the ice between the sticks of the players facing, no interference whatever allowed, before the puck has reached the ice. No player shall be allowed to come within five feet of players facing the puck.

Rule 3 (Time of Match and How Won): Three 20 minute periods of actual play, with 10 minutes intermission between, will be the time allowed for matches. Goals shall be changed after each period.

In case of a tie after playing the specified 60 minutes the teams shall immediately change goals, and play 10 minutes each way, or until one side shall have scored within the limits of such 20 minutes overtime. If at the end of 20 minutes the score is still tied, the match shall be called a draw. It is understood that any extra period played shall be considered part of the match and all unexpired penalties shall remain in force.

Rule 4 (Change of Players): Players may be changed at any time by the manager of the club, and said substitute shall be placed on the ice, and original player removed without interruption. (Change of players must only be made during temporary delay in the game.)

Unlimited player substitutions are allowed here, however changing on the fly is not. Substitutions could be made only during a stoppage.

Rule 5 (Injury to Players): In the event of a player being injured or compelled to leave the ice during a match, he may retire from the game and be replaced by a substitute, but play must continue without the teams leaving the ice.

In the event of a goal keeper sustaining an injury he will be allowed ten minutes to recuperate. In the event of him not being able to continue at the expiration of ten minutes his manager must put on a substitute.

Rule 6 (Face of Puck After Foul has Been Committed): Should the game be temporarily stopped by the infringement of any of the rules the puck must be taken back and faced where it was last played from before the infringement occurred. If, however, a foul occur within ten feet of the goal, the puck shall not be faced at the point where the foul occurred, but shall be taken to a point ten feet out from the goals and there faced.

Rule 7 (Face of Puck After Being Out of Bounds): When the puck goes off the ice or a foul occurs behind the goals, the puck shall be taken midway between the goal posts and the outside edge of the rink, on the side that it went out of bounds, and faced five yards at right angles from the goal line.

Rule 8 (Off-Side Play and Kicking Puck) : When a player hits the puck, any one of the same side who at such moment of hitting is nearer the opponent's goal-line, is out of play, and may not touch the puck himself or in any way whatever prevent any other player from doing so, until the puck has been played, except that in an area twenty feet each side of center line, which shall be marked off, this rule shall not apply. In the event of the puck rebounding off the goal keeper's body, skate or stick, players of his team touching puck will be considered on side.

No player shall kick the puck or hold the puck in his hands or carry it with any part of his body or raise his stick above his shoulders.

Rule 9 (Minor Fouls): A minor foul shall consist of holding an opponent or his stick, or tripping, when a goal is not in danger, loafing off side, off side interference, stopping of a goal by lying or kneeling on the ice.

For violation of the above a player shall be ruled off three minutes. Should a goal keeper stop a goal by deliberately falling or kneeling on the ice, he shall be warned for the first offence, and for each subsequent offence shall be ruled off for two minutes.

Loafing off-side – third offence shall constitute a major foul, and the penalty provided therefore shall apply.

The penalty rules have been revised to move away from the rather ridiculous 1911 practice of not producing a man-advantage situation, allowing a substitute for a the penalized player but collecting a fine from him. The player was punished, but the team was not. Now we're back to a situation that makes sense, sending penalized players off the ice without substitution.

Rule 10 (Major Fouls): A major foul shall consist of throwing a stick to prevent a score, tripping or holding an opponent or his stick to prevent a score, cross checking, charging from behind, forcibly body checking an opponent into the boards, hooking, cross checking, bodying or charging goal keeper, or interference by a substituting player before the player he is replacing is entirely out of play, loafing off side, after being penalized twice for the same offence as a minor foul, using foul or abusive language to any official or an attempt to injure an opposing player.

For the first offence the player shall be ruled off for five minutes, for the second offence, ten minutes; and for the third offence shall be ruled off for the remainder of the match.

When a player deliberately throws his stick to prevent a score, the referee shall immediately award a goal to the side offended against and the puck shall be faced and the game re-started as though a goal had actually been scored.

If any of the above fouls occur within the last ten minutes of playing time, the referee shall have the right to impose as an additional penalty, a fine not exceeding fifteen dollars.

Rule 11 (Match Foul): A match foul shall consist of deliberately injuring or disabling an opponent, or fighting.

For this offence a player shall be fined not less than fifteen dollars, and ruled off for such length of time as in the opinion of the referee shall constitute an adequate penalty, but in no case shall the player be allowed to return to the ice, without serving a penalty of at least ten minutes.

Any player incurring a second match foul in any one season shall automatically become suspended and shall not be permitted to play in any games until his case has been dealt with and his suspension lifted by the President of the Association.

In all cases where a player is ruled off, whether for a minor, major or a match foul, he shall be replaced by a substitute, and said substitute shall be placed on the ice without delay to the game.

Collection of Fines: Clubs to be immediately notified after each match by the Secretary of amount of fines levied. Fines to be deducted from the player on first following payment. Any clubs paying fine directly or indirectly for any players penalized shall be fined the sum of $200.00.

Rule 12 (How Goal Scored): A goal shall be scored when the puck shall have passed between the goal posts from in front and below the line drawn across the top of the posts, and across a dark line drawn from post to post, in or on the ice.

Rule 12(a): Should the puck be accidentally put through a goal by one of the players defending it, it shall be game for the team attacking that goal. Should it be put through a goal by any one not actually a player it shall not count.

Rule 13 (Goal Keeper): The goal keeper must not, during play, lie, kneel or sit upon the ice, but must maintain a standing position.

Rule 14 (Dimensions of Stick): Hockey sticks shall not be more than three inches wide at any part, with the exception of goal keeper's stick, which shall not exceed three-and-a-half inches.

Rule 15 (Dimensions of Puck): The puck must be made of vulcanized rubber, one inch all through and three inches in diameter.

The referee shall see that the official puck of this Association is used in all matches.

Rule 16 (Coaching): Coaching from the side of the rink through megaphones is absolutely prohibited.

In early organized hockey, the captain of a team would also essentially serve as its coach. References were made to James Creighton coaching his team on the ice in the very first matches. At this point in the game's history, regular player substitution was allowed for the first time. A captain, being subbed off, would presumably continue his coaching from the side. The rules allowed this, so long as he didn't make too much noise when doing so.

OHA Rules

When the Ontario Hockey Association (OHA) was organized in 1890, they drew up their own set of rules. These were largely based on the AHAC rules at the time (the 1886 code), but with some fairly significant differences, enough to cause some confusion when an AHAC team would go up against an OHA side in a match. The OHA rules were also used in Manitoba, and they spread West across Canada from there. Craig Bowlsby (2006) notes that early hockey in BC used the "Manitoba rules", and hockey in Manitoba at this time took its rules from the OHA. This is confirmed by the set of rules printed in the *Winnipeg Free Press* on March 5, 1892, which match this OHA code exactly.

The only 1886 AHAC rule that is not included in the first OHA code in some form is rule 1, which states that the captains select the two umpires and the referee. OHA rules specify that the referee appoints the umpire, and presumably the league reserved the right to name the referee for each match.

It is strange, given that hockey was introduced to Toronto (the centre of the OHA) by longtime Montreal player Tom Paton, that they should have a different set of laws for the game. We do know that organized hockey was played in Kingston in 1886, two years earlier than it was in Toronto. It's possible that the differences in rules originated there. At this time the origins are uncertain. However, as we can see in Appendix II, there is a strong possibility that the OHA offside rule was at least partly based on that of rugby football, rather than the Montreal rules of organized hockey.

1891 OHA RULES

Source: Slater (2012a).

Rule 1: The game is played on ice by teams of seven on each side, with a puck made of vulcanized rubber, one inch think all through and three inches in diameter. Hockey sticks shall not be more than three inches wide at any point.

A goal is placed in the middle of each goal line, composed of two upright posts, four feet in height, placed six feet apart, and at least five feet from the end of the ice.

The goal posts shall be firmly fixed. In the event of a goal being displaced or broken, the Referee shall blow his whistle and the game shall not proceed until the post is replaced.

The first section of this rule is 1886 AHAC Rule 12, Rule 11 and Rule 9 combined into one. The second section incorporates some of 1886 AHAC rule 4 for the dimensions of the net, and adds specifications for the construction of the goals and their distances from the ends of the rink.

The third section is new, though it surely is a simple codification of existing practice.

Rule 2: Each side shall have a captain (a member of his team), who, before the match, shall toss for choice of goals.

Each side shall play an equal time from each end. The duration of championship matches shall not be less than one hour, exclusive of stoppages. The team scoring the greater number of goals in that time shall be declared the winner of the match. If at the end of that time the game is a draw, ends will be changed, and the game continued until one side scores.

Tossing for choice of goals is not included in the AHAC rules, but was probably standard practice. 1886 AHAC Rule 13 is used for the length of a match, the victory condition and tie-breaker, with the added requirement for each side to play equal time from each end, which the Montreal rules would later incorporate.

Rule 3: There shall only be one referee for a match, and in no case shall he belong to either of the competing clubs. He shall enforce the rules, adjudicate upon disputes, or cases unprovided for by rule; appoint the goal umpires; keep the time and the score; and at the conclusion of the match declare the result. The puck shall be considered in play until the referee calls the game, which he may do at any time, and which he must do at once when any irregularity of play occurs, by sounding a whistle. His decision shall be final.

This is 1886 AHAC Rule 3, but with a great deal of additional, specific information about exactly what the referee has authority over during the game.

Rule 4: A goal shall be scored when the puck shall have passed between the goal posts from in front and below an imaginary line drawn across the tops of the posts.

Goal umpires shall inform the Referee when a goal is scored. Their decision shall be final.

The first section of this is 1886 AHAC Rule 10 (unchanged), while the second section is a reworded version of 1886 AHAC Rule 2.

Rule 5: The game shall be started and renewed by the referee calling play, after having placed the puck on its larger surface on the ice, between the sticks of two of the players, one from each team, who are to face it.

This is the first recorded codification of a faceoff procedure, and we can only assume it reflects existing practice. The language seems to suggest that the referee was to place the puck on the ice, and the two players taking the faceoff could not go for the puck until the referee called play.

However, it seems that in practice it meant the referee held the puck between the two players on the ice, and only removed his hand as he called play. In Young (1989, p. 87) it states that it was not until 1904 that the OHA, at referee Fred Waghorne's suggestion, adopted the modern practice of dropping the puck which was intended to spare the

98

referee from being whacked in the shins or the knuckles. The language of the rule suggests the referee could have placed the puck, moved away, and then called play, achieving the same effect. It's curious that this was not the practice.

It's also amusing that the rule spells out the puck is to be placed on its flat side, rather than its rounded edge, for the face. Were there any cases of a referee facing the puck on its edge? And if not, did the rulemakers really expect that any would?

Rule 6: A player is off-side when he is in front of the puck, or when the puck has been hit, touched or is being run with by any of his own side behind him (i.e, between himself and his own goal line.)

A player being off-side is put on-side when the puck has been hit by, or has touched the dress or person of any player of the opposite side, or when one of his own side has run in front of him, either with the puck or having played it when behind him.

If a player when off-side plays the puck, or annoys or obstructs an opponent, the puck shall be faced where it was last played before the off-side play occurred.

The offside rule is the most important rule in early organized hockey, and in the offside rule we find the only truly significant difference between the Montreal rules and the OHA. It's clear that this is intentional. Much of the original OHA code is obviously borrowed from the AHAC, based on the wording of many rules. But the offside rule here is completely original, and takes nothing from the AHAC wording. As such we can assume they intended for there to be differences, as indeed there are, however subtle they may be.

The crucial difference is that the OHA rule focuses on where a player is when he touches the puck, rather than the AHAC concern of where the player was when the puck was last struck. The player, if ahead of the puck, was offside but was not required to get himself back onside as in the AHAC with its "must always be own side of the puck" law. He can instead wait for the play catch up to him, which was known as "skating the player onside".

*Young (1989) points out that this allowed there to be "a play that had to be done slickly: an attacker was allowed to pass the puck ahead for a teammate as long **as he caught up to the puck by the time the teammate picked it up**..." [p. 28, emphasis in original])*

Note that, given the definition of a forward pass we dealt with earlier in the book (passing the puck to a player who is ahead of the passer at the time the pass is made), the OHA rules allowed a sort of forward pass, while the AHAC did not. In Ontario you could pass the puck to a player who is closer to the opponents' goal that you are, so long as by the time he gets the puck, you have caught him up.

Whenever an OHA team (or one from Manitoba) played an AHAC club, say for the Stanley Cup, the rules to be used would have to be decided. The differences in the offside rule would inevitably lead to a significant number of offside violations by the team not used to the rules being used, and sometimes even the referees would be confused.

Rule 7: The puck may not be stopped with the hand except by the goal-keeper (see Rule 9) but may be stopped, but not carried, or knocked on by any other part of the body. No player shall raise his stick above his shoulder. Charging from behind, tripping, collaring, kicking, cross-checking, or pushing shall not be allowed. And the referee may at his discretion, rule a player who has infringed the above rule, off the ice for the game in progress, or for the whole of that match.

This is from 1886 AHAC rule 6, except that skaters cannot stop puck with their hand, it removes shinning from the list of banned actions but adds cross-checking and pushing, and gives referees discretion in punishment instead of two warnings then sending off for the match.

There is evidence that this rule at least was used in Toronto before the formation of the OHA. In Slater (2012), there is a description of a match in February 1890 between the St. Georges and Granites, both of Toronto. The Granites' Billy Donaldson was sent off the ice for "a period of time". Under AHAC rules, this would have been impossible at the time, as a player sent off had to be sent off for the match if he was to be penalized at all. Under OHA rules, the referee had discretion. So this OHA rule, and indeed perhaps all of them, were likely codification of existing practice in this part of Ontario.

Indeed, in Slater (2012a), it is noted that the rules for the first OHA season were adopted "without much debate" which again suggests the organizers were familiar with the rules they were going to use.

Rule 8: When the puck goes off the ice behind the goal line, it shall be brought out by the referee, to a point five yards in front of the goal line, on a line at right angles thereto, from the point at which it left the ice, and there faced.

When the puck goes off the ice at the side, it shall be similarly faced three yards from the side.

This is part of 1886 AHAC Rule 7, with the distance changed to three yards from five yards.

Rule 9: The goal-keeper must not during play, lie, sit or kneel upon the ice; he may, when in goal, stop the puck with his hands, but shall not throw or hold it.

This is 1886 AHAC Rule 8, with the added specification that goalkeepers cannot throw or hold the puck. This is not really a new rule, since all players could stop the puck with their hand, but not play it with the hand. This is just being specific.

Rule 10: No change of players shall be made after a match has commenced, except by reason of accident or injury during the game.

Rule 11: Should any player be injured during a match and compelled to leave the ice, his side shall have the option of putting on a spare man from the reserve to equalize the teams. In the event of any dispute between the captains as to the injured player's fitness to continue the game, the matter shall at once be decided by the referee.

Rule 12: Should the game be stopped by the referee by reason of the infringement of any of the rules, or because of an accident or change of players, the puck shall be faced at the spot where it was last played, before such infringement, accident or change of players shall have occurred.

The above three rules are 1886 AHAC Rule 14, Rule 15 and Rule 16 respectively, all unchanged.

1893 OHA RULES

The OHA code of laws was revised before the 1893/94 season, with no truly significant changes.

Source: Slater, Kevin (2013). Season in Review Ontario Hockey Association 1893 – 1894. Blurb.com.

Rule 1: The game is played on ice by teams of seven on each side, with a puck made of vulcanized rubber, one inch think all through and three inches in diameter. Hockey sticks shall not be more than three inches wide at any part and not more than thirteen inches long in the blade.

A goal is placed in the middle of each goal line, composed of two upright posts, four feet in height, placed six feet apart, and at least five feet from the end of the ice.

The goal posts shall be firmly fixed. In the event of a goal being displaced or broken, the Referee shall blow his whistle and the game shall not proceed until the post is replaced.

This is 1891 OHA Rule 1, with the addition of the maximum length of the stick blade.

Rule 2: Each side shall play an equal time from each end. The duration of championship matches shall not be less than one hour, exclusive of stoppages. The team scoring the greater number of goals in that time shall be declared the winner of the match. If at the end of that time the game is a draw, ends will be changed, and the game continued until one side scores.

This is 1891 OHA Rule 2, however references to the teams having captains and tossing for the choice of goals has been deleted. Surely neither of these items actually disappeared from the game. In the next OHA rules revision they're explicitly stated once again.

Rule 3: Time-keepers shall be appointed, one by each captain to keep time during a match.

This is a new rule, which alleviates the referee of one of his numerous duties. Timekeepers did not appear until 1896 in the Montreal stream of rules, however we don't know for certain whether those rules were actually revised in 1896 or some season before, so we cannot say which was the first to include timekeepers.

Rule 4: There shall only be one referee for a match, and in no case shall he belong to either of the competing clubs. He shall enforce the rules, adjudicate upon disputes, or cases unprovided for by rule; appoint the goal umpires; control the time-keepers, keep the score, and at the conclusion of the match declare the result. The puck shall be considered in play until the referee stops the game, which he may do at any time, and which he must do at once when any irregularity of play occurs, by sounding a whistle. His decision shall be final.

This is 1891 OHA Rule 3, except the referee now has control over the timekeepers rather than keeping time himself.

Rule 5: A goal shall be scored when the puck shall have passed between the goal posts from in front and below an imaginary line drawn across the tops of the posts.

Goal umpires shall inform the referee when a goal is scored. Their decision shall be final.

Rule 6: The game shall be started and renewed by the referee calling 'play', after having placed the puck on its larger surface on the ice, between the sticks of two of the players, one from each team, who are to face it.

The above two rules are 1891 OHA Rule 4 and Rule 5, both unchanged.

Rule 7: A player shall always be on his own side of the puck. A player is off-side when he is in front of the puck, or when the puck has been hit, touched or is being run with by any of his own side behind him (ie, between himself and his own goal line.)

A player being off-side is put on-side when the puck has been hit by, or has touched the dress or person of any player of the opposite side, or when one of his own side has run in front of him, either with the puck or having played it when behind him.

If a player when off-side plays the puck, or annoys or obstructs an opponent, the puck shall be faced where it was last played before the off-side play occurred.

The offside rule is largely unchanged from 1891 OHA Rule 6, however the first sentence has been added from the Montreal Rules: "a player shall always be on his own side of the puck." This suggests that a player being offside was to try to get onside, rather than waiting for the play to catch up to him. Failing to do so would be considered loafing or lagging offside.

Rule 8: The puck may not be stopped with the hand except by the goal-keeper but may be stopped, but not carried, or knocked on by any other part of the body.

This is the first part of 1891 OHA Rule 7, unchanged.

Rule 9: No player shall raise his stick above his shoulder. Charging from behind, tripping, collaring, kicking, cross-checking, or pushing shall not be allowed. And the referee must rule off the ice, for any time in his discretion, a player who, in the opinion of the referee, has offended deliberately against this rule.

This is the second part of 1891 OHA Rule 7. The list of punishable offences is unchanged, however the application of penalties has changed. Previously the referee had the discretion to send off a man or not, and when doing so could do so for the game or the match. Now the referee is compelled to call a penalty, but has complete discretion as to its duration. Unlike the contemporary Montreal version of the rule, the referee was not required to warn a player once before issuing a penalty.

Rule 10: When the puck goes off the ice behind the goal line, it shall be brought out by the referee to a point five yards in front of the goal line, on a line at right angles thereto, from the point at which it left the ice, and there faced.

When the puck goes off the ice at the side, it shall be similarly faced three yards from the side.

This is 1891 OHA Rule 8, unchanged.

Rule 11: The goal-keeper must not during play, lie, sit or kneel upon the ice; he may when in goal, stop the puck with his hands, but shall not throw or hold it. The referee must rule off the ice, for any time in his discretion, a player who, in the opinion of the referee, has offended deliberately against this rule.

This is 1891 OHA Rule 9, with the additional provision of a penalty for an infraction.

Rule 12: No change of players shall be made after a match has commenced, except by reason of accident or injury during the game.

This is 1891 OHA Rule 10, unchanged.

Rule 13: Should any player be injured during a match and compelled to leave the ice, his side shall have the option of putting on a spare man from the reserve to equalize the teams. In the event of any dispute between the captains as to the injured player's fitness to continue the game, the matter shall at once be decided by the referee.

This is 1891 OHA Rule 11, changed so that the opposing team must drop a man instead of the team being allowed to put on a substitute.

Rule 14: Should the game be stopped by the referee by reason of the infringement of any of the rules, or because of an accident or change of players, the puck shall be faced at the spot where it was last played, before such infringement, accident or change of players shall have occurred.

This is 1891 OHA Rule 12, unchanged.

1899 OHA RULES

I refer to this code as the 1899 OHA rules, however this is based on the date of the source, which does not state when the revisions were adopted, and does not necessarily mean they were revised in 1899. The changes from the 1893 version of the rules are minor.

Source: Farrell (1899).

Rule 1 (Game): The game is played on ice by teams of seven on each side, with a puck made of vulcanized rubber, one inch think all through and three inches in diameter.

This is the first part of 1893 OHA Rule 1, unchanged.

Rule 2 (Sticks): Hockey sticks shall not be more than three inches wide at any part, and not more than thirteen inches long in the blade.

This is the second part of 1893 OHA Rule 1, unchanged.

Rule 3 (Goal): A goal is placed in the middle of each goal line, composed of two upright posts, four feet in height, placed six feet apart, and at least five feet from the end of the ice.

The goal posts shall be firmly fixed. In the event of a goal being displaced or broken, the Referee shall blow his whistle and the game shall not proceed until the post is replaced.

This is the third and fourth parts of 1893 OHA Rule 1.

Rule 4 (Match): Each side shall have a captain (a member of his team) who, before the match, shall toss for choice of goals.

This is the first part of 1891 OHA Rule 2, which had been deleted from the 1893 version of the OHA rules, but added back again here.

Rule 5: Each side shall play an equal time from each end. The duration of championship matches shall not be less than one hour, exclusive of stoppages. The team scoring the greater number of goals in that time shall be declared the winner of the match. If at the end of that time the game is a draw, ends will be changed and the game continued for ten minutes, each side playing five minutes from each end with a rest of five minutes between, and if neither side has scored a majority of games, similar periods of ten minutes shall be played in the same way until one side shall have scored a majority of goals.

This is 1893 OHA Rule 2, however the overtime procedure has changed. Whereas the previous rules called for unlimited sudden-death overtime, the rules now call for 10-minute periods of overtime, not sudden-death.

Rule 6 (Time-Keepers): Time-keepers shall be appointed, one by each captain, to keep the time during match.

Rule 7 (Referee): There shall only be one Referee for a match, and in no case shall he belong to either of the competing clubs. He shall enforce the rules, adjudicate upon disputes or cases unprovided for by rule; appoint the goal Umpires; control the Time-keepers; keep the score; and at the conclusion of the match declare the result. The puck shall be considered in play until the referee calls the game, which he may do at any time, and which he must do at once when any irregularity of play occurs, by sounding a whistle. His decision shall be final.

The two rules above are 1893 OHA Rule 3 amd Rule 4 respectively, both unchanged.

Rule 8 (Score): A goal shall be scored when the puck shall have passed between the goal posts from in front and below an imaginary line drawn across the tops of the posts.

Rule 9 (Goal Umpires): Goal umpires shall inform the Referee when a goal is scored. Their decision shall be final.

The above two rules are 1893 OHA Rule 5, broken into two parts.

Rule 10 (Face): The game shall be started and renewed by the Referee calling "play", after having placed the puck on its larger surface on the ice, between the sticks of two of the players, one from each team, who are to face it. After a goal has been scored the puck shall be played on the centre of the ice.

This is 1893 OHA Rule 6, with the additional provision that a face takes place at centre ice after a goal, which was surely the existing practice.

Rule 11 (Off-Side): A player shall always be on his side of the puck. A player is off-side when he is in front of the puck, or when the puck has been hit, touched or is being run with by any of his own side behind him (i.e, between himself and the end of the rink near which his goal is placed.)

A player being off-side is put on-side when the puck has been hit by, or has touched the dress or person of any player of the opposite side, or when one of his own side has run in front of him, either with the puck or having played when behind him.

If a player when off-side plays the puck, or annoys or obstructs an opponent, the puck shall be faced where it was last played before the off-side play occurred.

Rule 12 (Knocking-On): The puck may not be stopped with the hand except by the goal-keeper but may be stopped, but not carried, or knocked on by any other part of the body.

Rule 13 (Charging, Tripping, Etc.): No player shall raise his stick above his shoulder. Charging from behind, tripping, collaring, kicking, cross-checking, or pushing shall not be allowed. And the Referee must rule off the ice, for any time in his discretion, a player who, in the opinion of the Referee, has deliberately offended against the above rule.

Rule 14 (When the Puck Leaves the Ice): When the puck goes off the ice behind the goal line, it shall be brought out by the referee, to a point five yards in front of the goal line, on a line at right angles thereto, from the point at which it left the ice, and there faced.

When the puck goes off the ice at the side, it shall be similarly faced three yards from the side.

The four rules above are 1893 OHA Rule 7 through Rule 10 respectively, all unchanged.

Rule 15 (Goal-Keeper): The goal-keeper must not during play, lie, sit or kneel upon the ice; he may, when in goal, stop the puck with his hands, but shall not throw or hold it. He may wear pads, but must not wear a garment such as would give him undue assistance in keeping goal. The Referee must rule off the ice, for any time in his discretion, a player who, in the opinion of the Referee, has offended deliberately against this rule.

The restrictions on the goaltender have been expanded from 1893 OHA Rule 11. This the first reference to a goaltender wearing pads, which was initiated by Winnipeg's Whitey Merritt. It also bars any garment that gives "undue" assistance in keeping goal, whatever that's supposed to mean. Presumably a garment that serves to protect the goaltender's vital parts from the hard rubber puck is fine, but not one that is only designed to stop the puck from entering the goal. Goalie pads started out quite narrow, serving principally to protect the netminder's poor shins, but by the late 1910s they had become much wider, obviously intended more to assist in stopping the puck than in mere bruise prevention.

Rule 16 (Change of Players): No change of players shall be made after a match has commenced, except by reason of accident or injury during the game.

Rule 17 (Injured Player): Should any player be injured during a match, break his skate, or from any other accident and compelled to

111

leave the ice, the opposite side shall immediately drop a man to equalize the teams. In the event of any dispute, the matter shall at once be decided by the Referee.

Rule 18 (Stoppages): Should the game be stopped by the Referee by reason of the infringement of any of the rules, or because of an accident or change of players, the puck shall be faced at the spot where it was last played, before such infringement, accident or change of players shall have occurred.

The above three rules are 1893 OHA Rule 12, Rule 13 and Rule 14 respectively, all unchanged.

1900 OHA RULES

The OHA rules were revised before the 1900/01 season, however only two small changes were made.

Source: The Ontario Hockey Association. Constitution, Rules of Competition and Laws of the Game as Amended Dec. 1st, 1900.

Rule 1 (Game): The game is played on ice by teams of seven on each side, with a puck made of vulcanized rubber, one inch think all through and three inches in diameter.

Rule 2 (Sticks): Hockey sticks shall not be more than three inches wide at any part, and not more than thirteen inches long in the blade.

Rule 3 (Goal): A goal is placed in the middle of each goal line, composed of two upright posts, four feet in height, placed six feet apart, and at least five feet from the end of the ice. The goal posts shall be firmly fixed. In the event of a goal being displaced or broken, the Referee shall blow his whistle and the game shall not proceed until the post is replaced.

Rule 4 (Match): Each side shall have a captain (a member of his team), who, before the match, shall toss for choice of goals.

Rule 5: Each side shall play an equal time from each end. The duration of championship matches shall not be less than one hour, exclusive of stoppages. The team scoring the greater number of goals in that time shall be declared the winner of the match. If at the end of that time the game is a draw, ends shall be changed and the game continued for ten minutes, each side playing five minutes from each end with a rest of five minutes between, and if neither side has scored a majority of games, similar periods of ten minutes shall be payer in the same way until one side shall have scored a majority of goals.

Rule 6 (Time-Keepers): Time-keepers shall be appointed, one by each captain, to keep the time during match.

Rule 7 (Referee): There shall only be one Referee for a match, and in no case shall he belong to either of the competing clubs. He shall enforce the rules, adjudicate upon disputes or cases unprovided for by rule; appoint the goal Umpires; control the Time-keepers; keep the score; and at the conclusion of the match declare the result. The puck shall be considered in play until the Referee stops the game, which he may do at any time, and which he must do at once when any irregularity of play occurs, by sounding a whistle. His decision shall be final.

Rule 8 (Score): A goal shall be scored when the puck shall have passed between the goal posts from in front and below an imaginary line drawn across the tops of the posts.

Rule 9 (Goal Umpires): Goal Umpires shall inform the Referee when a goal is scored. Their decision shall be final.

Rule 10 (Face): The game shall be started and renewed by the Referee calling "Play" after having placed the puck on its larger surface on the ice, between the sticks of two of the players, one from each team, who are to face it. After a goal has been scored the puck shall be played on the centre of the ice.

Rule 11 (Off-Side): A player shall always be on his side of the puck. A player is off-side when he is in front of the puck, or when the puck has been hit, touched or is being run with, by any of his own side behind him (i.e, between himself and the end of the rink near which his goal is placed.)

A player being off-side is put on-side when the puck has been hit by, or has touched the dress or person of any player of the opposite side, or when one of his own side has run in front of him, either with the puck or having played it when behind him.

If a player when off-side plays the puck, or annoys or obstructs an opponent, the puck shall be faced where it was last played before the off-side play occurred.

The above 11 rules are 1899 OHA Rule 1 through Rule 11 respectively, all unchanged.

Rule 12 (Knocking-On): The puck may be stopped with the hand but not carried or held or knocked on by any other part of the body.

This is 1899 OHA Rule 12, however the ability to stop the puck with the hand is no longer restricted to goaltenders. This brings the OHA rules in line with the contemporary Montreal version.

Rule 13 (Charging, Tripping, Etc.): No player shall raise his stick above his shoulder. Charging from behind, tripping, collaring, kicking, cross-checking, or pushing shall not be allowed. And the Referee must rule off the ice, for any time in his discretion, a player who, in the opinion of the Referee, has deliberately offended against the above rule.

Rule 14 (When the Puck Leaves the Ice): When the puck goes off the ice behind the goal line it shall be brought out by the Referee to a point five yards in front of the goal line, on a line at right angles thereto, from the point at which it left the ice, and there faced.

When the puck goes off the ice at the side, it shall be similarly faced three yards from the side.

Rule 15 (Goal-Keeper): The goal-keeper must not during play, lie, sit or kneel upon the ice; he may, when in goal, stop the puck with his hands, but shall not throw or hold it. He may wear pads, but must not wear a garment such as would give him undue assistance in keeping goal. The Referee must rule off the ice, for any time in his discretion, a player who, in the opinion of the Referee, has offended deliberately against this rule.

The above three rules are 1899 OHA Rule 13, Rule 14 and Rule 15 respectively, all unchanged.

Rule 16 (Change of Players): No change of players shall be made after a match has commenced, except by reason of accident or injury during the game. Should any player be injured during a match, break his skate, or from any other accident be compelled to leave the ice, the opposite side shall immediately drop a man to equalize the teams and the match proceed, without such players until such time as the player so compelled to leave the ice is ready to return. In the event of any dispute, the matter shall at once be decided by the Referee.

This is a combination of 1899 OHA Rule 16 and Rule 17, with the additional note that the opposing side only drops a player until the other player is ready to return to the ice.

Rule 17 (Stoppages): Should the game be stopped by the Referee by reason of the infringement of any of the rules, or because of an accident or change of players, the puck shall be faced at the spot where it was last played, before such infringement, accident or change of players shall have occurred.

This is 1899 OHA Rule 18, unchanged.

1905 OHA RULES

The OHA code was amended on November 11, 1905 to add a number of rule changes. Most are simply expansions, clarifications or refinements of existing rules, however there is a very important exception added to the offside rule.

Source: The Ontario Hockey Association. History and Constitution, Rules of Competition and Laws of the Game as Amended November 11, 1905.

Rule 1: The game is played on ice by teams of seven on each side, with a puck made of vulcanized rubber, one inch think all through and three inches in diameter.

This is 1900 OHA Rule 1, unchanged.

Rule 2 (Sticks): Hockey sticks shall not be more than three inches wide at any part, and not more than thirteen inches long in the blade. They shall consist entirely of wood, with tape binding permissible.

This is 1900 OHA Rule 2, with added detail about the permitted construction of the stick.

Rule 3 (Goal): A goal is placed in the middle of each goal line, composed of official goal nets supported by two upright posts, four feet in height, placed six feet apart, and at least five feet from the end of the ice. The goal posts shall be firmly fixed. In the event of a goal being displaced or broken, the Referee shall blow his whistle and the game shall not proceed until the post is replaced. It shall be the duty of the referee before each match to measure the goals.

This is 1900 OHA Rule 3, with the added provisions that the referee is to measure the goals before a match, and that goal nets are to be used.

Rule 4 (Match): Each side shall have a captain (a member of his team), who, before the match, shall toss for choice of goals.

Rule 5: Each side shall play an equal time from each end. The duration of championship matches shall not be less than one hour, exclusive of stoppages. The team scoring the greater number of goals in that time shall be declared the winner of the match, subject to the qualifications contained in Rules of Competition, No. 15. If at the end of that time the game is a draw, ends shall be changed and the game continued for ten minutes, each side playing five minutes from each end with a rest of five minutes between, and if neither side has scored a majority of games, similar periods of ten minutes shall be payer in the same way until one side shall have scored a majority of goals.

This is 1900 OHA Rule 5, with the addition of a reference to Rules of Competition. These rules are administrative matters for the OHA, and do not affect the game as played on the ice. The particular rule referred to here reads:

"15. In two-club groups where home and home matches are played, including the play-off of the different group winners in the semi-finals and finals, one hour's play only shall constitute each match, and a majority of goals in both matches shall decide the winner. In case of both clubs scoring an equal number of goals in the two matches there shall be a third and decisive game on neutral ice, time and place to be fixed by the Executive. In groups of three or more clubs a majority of matches shall decide the winner. Every match, except as hereinbefore provided, shall be played to a finish, as provided in No. 5 of the Rules of the game. [ie, 1905 OHA Rule 5]"

Rule 6 (Time-Keepers): Two time-keepers shall be appointed, one by each captain, before the commencement of the match, whose duty it shall be to keep an accurate account of the time of each game, deducting time for stoppages in the actual play. They shall immediately report to the referee any variance in their time, and the matter shall be at once decided by him. The referee also shall appoint a time-keeper, who shall keep the time of penalized players, and shall direct them to enter the game. The time-keepers shall be under the control of the referee. A gong shall be kept for their use.

1900 OHA Rule 6 has been greatly expanded here, providing additional timekeepers and much more detail as to the responsibilities of the timekeepers. There is now a specific penalty timekeeper.

Rule 7 (Referee): There shall only be one referee for a match, and in no case shall he belong to either of the competing clubs, and he may be an amateur or a professional. He is to enforce the rules; adjudicate upon disputes or cases unprovided for by rule; appoint or remove goal umpires; control the time-keepers; keep the score, announcing each goal as scored; and at the conclusion of the match declare the result. The puck shall be considered in play until the referee stops the game, which he may do at any time, and which he must do at once when any irregularity of play occurs, by sounding a whistle. His decision shall be final.

This is 1900 OHA Rule 7, with the noteworthy addition that while professional hockey players were abhorrent to the league, professional hockey referees were just fine. Surely if professional players would be subject to the evil effects of money, referees would be as well? The rules against professionalism were always more driven by ideology than reason, and this is good example of this inconsistency.

Rule 8 (Score): A goal shall be scored when the puck shall have passed between the goal posts from in front and below the tops of the posts.

With the introduction of goal nets, the reference to an imaginary line across the top of the goal posts in 1900 OHA Rule 8 is removed.

Rule 9 (Goal Umpires): There shall be one goal umpire at each goal; they shall inform the referee when the puck has been put into the goal from the front.

1900 OHA Rule 9 is reworded to the same effect; however this does render Rule 8 rather redundant.

Rule 10 (Face): The game shall be started and renewed by the Referee calling "Play" after dropping the puck in the centre of the ice between the sticks of two players, one from each team, who are to face it. After a goal has been scored the puck shall be faced in like manner on the centre of the ice.

Here we see the first mention of a referee dropping the puck rather than placing it on the ice for a faceoff. This innovation is credited to referee Fred Waghorne.

Rule 11 (Off-Side): A player shall always be on his side of the puck. A player is off-side when he is in front of the puck, or when the puck has been hit, touched or is being run with, by any of his own side behind him (i.e, between himself and the end of the rink near which his goal is placed.)

A player being off-side is put on-side when the puck has been hit by, or has touched the dress or person of any player of the opposite side, or when one of his own side has run in front of him, either with the puck or having played it when behind him.

If a player when off-side plays the puck, or annoys or obstructs an opponent, the puck shall be faced where it was last played before the off-side play occurred. A player on the defending side shall not be off-side when he takes a pass from or plays the puck as it bounds off his goal-keeper within a space of three feet out from goal and extending to the side of the rink.

An exception is added to 1900 OHA Rule 11 for defensive players touching the puck when it comes off their goaltender, if they are close enough to the net. Previously such an act would render the defensive player offside, meaning that defenders could not touch rebounds while offensive players could. See the discussion under 1877 Montreal Rule 2.

Rule 12 (Knocking-On): The puck may be stopped with the hand but not carried or held or knocked on by any other part of the body.

This is 1900 OHA Rule 12, unchanged.

Rule 13 (Charging, Tripping, Etc.): No player shall raise his stick above his shoulder. Charging from behind, tripping, collaring, kicking, cross-checking, or pushing shall not be allowed. And the referee must rule off the ice, for any time in his discretion, a player who, in the opinion of the Referee, has deliberately offended against the above rule. If a player makes any unfair or rough play, or disputes any decision of the referee or uses any foul or abusive language, the referee may rule him off for the remainder of the game or for such time as he may deem expedient, and no substitute shall be allowed.

1900 OHA Rule 13 is added to here, specifying that players cannot cuss or argue with the referee. Also, this is the first reference to a rough play penalty, which we simply call roughing now.

Rule 14 (When the Puck Leaves the Ice): When the puck goes off the ice behind the goal line it shall be brought out by the Referee to a point five yards in front of the goal line, on a line at right angles thereto, from the point at which it left the ice, and there faced.

When the puck goes off the ice at the side, it shall be similarly faced three yards from the side.

Rule 15 (Goal-Keeper): The goal-keeper must not during play, lie, sit or kneel upon the ice; he may stop the puck with his hands, but shall not throw or hold it. He may wear pads, but must not wear a garment such as would give him undue assistance in keeping goal. The Referee must rule off the ice, for any time in his discretion, a player who, in the opinion of the Referee, has offended deliberately against this rule.

The above two rules are 1900 OHA Rule 14 and Rule 15 respectively, both unchanged.

Rule 16 (Change of Players): No change of players shall be made after a match has commenced. Should any player be injured during a match, break his skate, or from any other accident be compelled to leave the ice, the opposite side shall immediately drop a man to equalize the teams and the match proceed, without such players until such time as the player so compelled to leave the ice is ready to return. In the event of any dispute, the matter shall at once be decided by the Referee.

This is 1900 OHA Rule 16, but now specifying there are no substitutions to be allowed at all. The only option in case of injury or similar incident is to drop the player from your side.

Rule 17 (Stoppages): Should any match be stopped by the referee by reason of the infringement of any of the rules, or because of an accident or change of players, the puck shall be faced at the spot where it was last played, before such infringement, accident or change of players shall have occurred.

This is 1900 Rule 17, slightly reworded. Note that even though no change of players is now allowed, the reference to such a change remains here.

1895 NEW BRUNSWICK RULES

Organized hockey was played in New Brunswick from at least 1894. Farrell (1899) makes reference to Montreal teams having travelled to the Maritimes in the 1890s, and noted that the quality of the teams there was already quite good by that time:

"In the Maritime Provinces, hockey has been introduced to stay...in fact, the senior teams of Halifax and St. John, in virtue of their showing against sevens that have visited them from Montreal, are eligible to compete for the Stanley Cup."

The rules of the City Amateur Hockey League of Saint John, New Brunswick, are presented here to give an idea of how organized hockey was being played in New Brunswick in 1895. The code is a lightly-edited version of the 1893 AHAC rules.

Source: Constitution By-Laws and Rules of the City Amateur Hockey League of St. John, 1895.

Rule 1 (Team): A Team shall be composed of seven players, who shall be bone-fide members of the clubs they represent and also bona fide residents of St. John. No player shall be allowed to play on more than one team in the same series during a season.

The only difference between this and 1893 AHAC Rule 1 is the addition that the players must be legitimate residents of Saint John, and there is no exception for playing on more than one team with a change in residence.

Rule 2 (Game): The game shall be commenced and renewed by a face in the centre of the rink. Rink must be at least 112 feet by 58 feet, or as near as this size as possible.

A bit of wording is added to 1893 AHAC Rule 2 "or as near this size as possible," thus rendering the "at least" part rather ineffectual.

Rule 3 (Goals): Goals shall be six feet wide and four feet high.

Rule 4 (Face): The puck shall be faced by being placed between the sticks of two opponents, and the Referee then calling "play." The goals shall be placed at least ten feet from the edge of the ice.

Rule 5 (Match): Two half hours, with an intermission of ten minutes between, will be the time allowed for matches, but no stops of more than fifteen minutes will be allowed. A match will be decided by the team winning the greatest numbers of games during that time. In case of a tie after playing the specified two half hours, play will continue until one side secures a game, unless otherwise agreed upon between the captains before the match. Goals shall be changed after each half hour.

The above three rules are 1893 AHAC Rule 3, Rule 4 and Rule 5, all unchanged.

Rule 6 (Change of Players): No change of players shall be made after a match has commenced, except for reasons of accidents or injury during the game, or for other reasons satisfactory to the referee.

The referee is given some discretion in allowing for a player to be substituted, beyond what is prescribed by 1893 AHAC Rule 6.

Rule 7: Should any player be injured during a match and compelled to leave the ice, his side shall have the option of putting on a spare man from the reserve to equalize the teams; in the event of any dispute between the captains as to the injured player's fitness to continue the game, the matter shall be decided by the Referee.

Here, rather than adopting 1893 AHAC Rule 7, 1886 AHAC Rule 15 is used such that there is no second-half option of dropping a player.

Rule 8 (Stoppages): Should a game be temporarily stopped by the infringement of any of the rules, the captain of the opposite team may claim that the puck be taken back and a face take place where it was last played from before such infringement occurred.

Rule 9 (Off-Side): When a player hits the puck, any one of the same side who at such moment of hitting is nearer the opponent's goal line is out of play, and may not touch the puck himself, or in any way whatever prevent any other player from doing so until the puck has been played. A player must always be on his own side of the puck.

The two above rules are 1893 AHAC Rule 8 and Rule 9, both unchanged.

Rule 10 (Knocking on, Charging, Etc.): The puck may be stopped, but not carried or knocked on, by any part of the body. No player shall raise his stick above his shoulder except in lifting the puck. Charging from behind, tripping, collaring, kicking or shinning shall not be allowed, and any player after having been warned by the Referee, he may be ruled off the ice for that game or match.

Once again, rather than using 1893 AHAC Rule 10, 1886 AHAC Rule 6 is partly the basis here, as there is no lifting exception to the high-sticking rule. The referee does not have full discretion in penalty times; it's either the game or the match.

Rule 11 (Puck Off Ice): When the puck goes off the ice or a foul occurs behind the goals it shall be taken by the Referee to five yards at right angles from the goal line and there faced. When the puck goes off the ice at the sides it shall be taken three yards at right angles from the boundary line and there faced.

This is almost identical to 1893 AHAC Rule 11, however the OHA standard of three yards for pucks off at the side is used instead of five yards.

Rule 12 (Goal-keeper): The goal-keeper must not, during play, lie, kneel or sit upon the ice, but must maintain a standing position.

Rule 13 (Score): A goal shall be scored when the puck shall have passed between the goal posts from in front below an imaginary line across the top of posts.

Rule 14 (Sticks): Hockey sticks shall not be more than three inches wide at any point.

Rule 15 (Puck): The puck must be made of vulcanized rubber, one inch all through and three inches in diameter.

The four rules above are 1893 AHAC Rule 12 through Rule 15 respectively, all unchanged.

Rule 16 (Officials): The captains of the contesting teams shall agree upon a Referee and two Umpires at least twenty-four hours before a match; failing to agree the Executive Committee shall appoint both. Umpires: one shall stand behind each goal, which position they will retain until close of match.

This modified version of 1893 AHAC Rule 16 puts the power to appoint officials in the hands of the league executive if agreement is not made by the team captains. It also makes no mention of a timekeeper; presumably the referee was expected to keep the time.

Rule 17 (Referee): All disputes on the ice shell be settled by the Referee, and his decision shall be final.

This is 1893 AHAC Rule 17, unchanged.

Rule 18 (Umpires): All questions as to games shall be settled by the Umpires, and their decisions shall be final. In the event of any dispute as to the decision of an Umpire the Referee shall have power to remove and replace him.

This is 1886 AHAC Rule 2 rather than 1893 AHAC Rule 18, in that the referee does not have the power to remove an umpire.

United States

Organized hockey came to the United States of America in the mid-1890s. Leagues were formed in both New York and Pittsburgh before the turn of the century, and organized hockey also began to be played around 1895 in the Twin Cities in Minnesota. The following section discusses the codes of law of the American Amateur Hockey League (AAHL), based in New York, the rules of which were largely based on the Montreal lineage of rules, as it was Canadian clubs travelling from Montreal to play exhibitions in New York that helped popularize the sport there.

I have not found a set of printed rules for the Western Pennsylvania Hockey League (WPHL), which was originally formed around the same time as the AAHL. However, as noted in Slater (2010), it was in 1895 that the Queen's University hockey club, touring from Kingston, introduced the Canadian game to Pittsburgh, where they had been playing ice polo. Queen's returned for a series of games in 1899 against WPHL clubs, and no mention was made of significant rule differences between the teams, so it should be safe to assume that the WPHL was using OHA rules as Queen's did. Similarly, Minnesota imported hockey from Manitoba, and senior Winnipeg sides played matches there in 1895 and 1896, so we can safely say that they used OHA rules in Minneapolis and St. Paul as well, since that's what the Manitoba clubs were using.

1896 AAHL RULES

In 1896, the AAHL began play in New York. The code of this league was based on the 1893 version of the AHAC rules. We can see this because the rules are presented in exactly the same order, and most of them are copied verbatim. Interestingly, though, they writers of this code also considered the 1891 OHA rules, and incorporated a few bits they liked from that code.

Many, if not most, of the players in the AAHL were Canadian imports, and certainly nearly all of the best players were from north of the border. Most of these came from the Montreal Rules territory, though there were some from the OHA as well. So it makes sense that the rules would primarily be drawn from the AHAC.

Source: Farrell (1899).

Rule 1 (Team): A team shall be composed of seven players, who shall be bona-fide members of the club they represent.

This is 1893 AHAC Rule 1, but without the explicit prohibition of a player playing for more than one club in a season.

Rule 2 (Game): The game shall be commenced and renewed by a face in the centre of the rink. Rink shall be at least 112 feet by 58 feet.

This is 1893 AHAC Rule 2, unchanged.

Rule 3 (Goals): A goal is placed in the middle of each goal line, composed of two upright posts, four feet in height, placed six feet apart, and at least five feet from the end of the ice. The goal posts should be firmly fixed. In the event of a goal post being displaced or broken, the Referee shall blow his whistle, and the game shall not proceed until the goal is replaced.

This is made up of the second and third parts of 1893 OHA Rule 1.

Rule 4 (Face): The puck shall be faced by being placed between the stick of two opponents, and the Referee then calling play.

This is 1893 AHAC Rule 4, but without the specification of where the goals are to be placed, which is covered in Rule 3 above.

Rule 5 (Match): Two halves of twenty minutes each, exclusive of stoppages, with an intermission of ten minutes between, will be the time allowed for games. A game will be decided by the team scoring the greatest number of goals during that time. In case of a tie after playing the specified time, play will continue for ten minutes more, when, in the event of the score still being even, another game will be played at a time and place mutually agreed upon, such time to be prior to the next scheduled game. Goals shall be changed after each half.

This is based on 1893 AHAC Rule 5, but the matches are shorter and overtime is limited to 10 minutes. Ice time was in relatively short supply for the AAHL; games in New York were played at the brand new St. Nicholas Rink and hockey did not have the importance it did in Canada.

Tie games after overtime were not to be counted in the standings, instead being replayed.

Rule 6 (Change of Players): No change of players shall be made after a game has commenced, except for reasons of accidents or injury during the game.

This is 1893 AHAC Rule 6, unchanged.

Rule 7: Should any player meet with an accident during a game and be compelled to leave the ice, his side shall have the option of putting on a spare man from the reserve to equalize the teams. In the event of any dispute between the captains as to such player's fitness to continue the game, the matter shall at once be decided by the Referee.

This is 1886 AHAC Rule 15 or 1893 OHA Rule 13, and not 1893 AHAC Rule 7 as one might expect. The difference is that there is no option for the other team to drop a man rather than having a sub come on.

Rule 8 (Stoppages): Should a game be temporarily stopped by the infringement of any of the rules, the captain of the opposite team may claim that the puck be taken back and a face take place where it was last played from before such infringement occurred.

Rule 9 (Off-Side): When a player hits the puck, any one of the same side who at such moment of hitting is nearer the opponent's goal is offside, and may not touch the puck himself or in any way whatever prevent any other player from doing so until the puck has been played. A player must always be on his own side of the puck.

The above two rules are 1893 AHAC Rule 8 and Rule 9 respectively, both unchanged.

Rule 10 (Knocking on, Charging, Etc.): The puck may be stopped, but not carried not knocked on, by any part of the body. No player shall raise his stick above the shoulder. Charging from behind, tripping, collaring, kicking or cross-checking shall not be allowed, and the Referee must rule off the ice, for any time in his discretion, a player who, in his opinion has offended deliberately against the above rule.

This rule is a bit of a mishmash. Its wording at the beginning is from 1893 AHAC Rule 10, however it does not contain the high-sticking exception for lifting, so it's more like 1886 AHAC Rule 6. However it also removes shinning from the list of offences, and adds cross-checking from 1893 OHA Rule 9, and from that same rule the referee is not required to warn a player before sending him off, and uses the same "offended deliberately" language.

Rule 11 (Puck Off Ice): When the puck goes off the ice behind the goal line, or a foul occurs behind the goal line, the puck shall be brought by the Referee to a point five yards in front of the goal line, at right angles from the point at which it left the ice, and there faced. When the puck goes off the ice at the side it shall be similarly faced three yards from the side.

This is 1891 OHA Rule 8, due to where the puck is faced after going off the side.

Rule 12 (Goal-keeper): The goal-keeper must not, during play, lie, kneel or sit upon the ice, but must maintain a standing position.

Rule 13 (Score): A goal shall be scored when the puck shall have passed between the goal posts from in front and below an imaginary line across the top of posts.

The above two rules are 1893 AHAC Rule 12 and Rule 13 respectively, both unchanged.

Rule 14 (Sticks): Hockey sticks shall be made of wood, with no harder substance attached thereto, and shall not be more than three inches wide at any point.

While based on 1893 AHAC Rule 14, the AAHL code is unique in stating that the sticks must be made of wood, and that no substance harder than wood can be attached to them.

Rule 15 (Puck): The puck must be made of vulcanized rubber, one inch thick all through and three inches in diameter.

This is 1893 AHAC Rule 15, unchanged.

Rule 16 (Officials): The captains of the contesting teams shall agree upon a Referee, a Timekeeper and two Umpires, one to be stationed behind each goal, which positions shall not be changed during a game except by mutual consent.

This is based on 1893 AHAC Rule 16, however reducing the number of timekeepers to one.

Rule 17 (Referee): All disputes on the ice shall be settled by the Referee, and his decision shall be final.

Rule 18 (Umpires): All questions as to goals shall be settled by the Umpires, and their decisions shall be final.

These final two rules are 1893 AHAC Rule 17 and Rule 18 respectively, both unchanged.

1901 AAHL RULES

The AAHL amended its rules before the 1900/01 season, for the most part simply moving closer to the CAHL rules of the time. However, there are some other significant changes as well.

Source: Farrell, Art (1901). Spalding's Athletic Library Ice Hockey and Ice Polo Guide. New York: American Sports Publishing Co.

Rule 1: A team shall be composed of seven players, who shall be *bona-fide* members of the club they represent. No player shall be allowed to play on more than one team in the same series during a season.

This is 1896 AAHL Rule 1, but adding the restriction on a player playing for more than one side in a season, bringing it fully in line with 1893 AHAC Rule 1.

Rule 2: The game shall be commenced and renewed by a face in the centre of the rink. Rink shall be at least 112 feet by 58 feet.

Goals shall be 6 feet wide and 4 feet high.

The puck shall be faced by being placed between the stick of two opponents, and the Referee then calling play.

The goals shall be placed at least ten feet form the edge of the ice.

The AAHL switched from using the 1891 OHA code to the 1893 AHAC laws for the basis of this rule. This rule combines 1893 AHAC Rule 2, Rule 3 and Rule 4. It makes no real change, but removes some of the specificity included in the OHA version.

Rule 3: Two 20-minute halves, with an intermission of ten minutes between, will be the time allowed for matches, but no stops of more than five (5) minutes will be allowed. A match will be decided by the team winning the greatest number of games during that time. In case of a tie after playing the specified two 20-minutes halves, play will continue until one side secures a game, unless otherwise agreed upon between the captains before the match. Goals shall be changed after each half.

This is 1896 AAHL Rule 5, however the reference to the time being exclusive of stoppages is removed, and a limit of 5 minutes is placed on stoppages. This suggests the AAHL may have started using straight-time for their matches rather than stop-time. Again this would reflect the limited ice time available to hockeyists in New York. The limit on overtime, and the requirement to replay tied games, have both been removed.

Rule 4: No change of players shall be made after a game has commenced, except for reasons of accidents or injury during the game.

This is 1896 AAHL Rule 6, unchanged.

Rule 5: Should any player be injured during the first half of a match and compelled to leave the ice, his side shall be allowed to put on a spare man from the reserve to equalize the teams; should any player be injured during the second half of the match, the captain of the opposing team shall have the option of dropping a player to equalize the teams or allow his opponents to put on a man from the reserve. In the event of any dispute between the captains as to the injured player's fitness to continue the game, the matter shall at once be decided by the Referee.

Once again the AAHL makes an edit to bring its code more in line with the 1893 AHAC Rules, in this case by using 1893 AHAC Rule 7 with some minor rewording which does not change its meaning.

Rule 6: Should the game be temporarily stopped by the infringement of any of the rules, the captain of the opposite team may claim that the puck be taken back and a face take place where it was last played from before such infringement occurred.

This is 1896 AAHL Rule 8, unchanged.

Rule 7: When a player hits the puck, anyone of the same side, who at such moment of hitting is nearer the opponent's goal is out of play, and may not touch the puck himself or in any way whatever prevent any other player from doing so until the puck has been played. A player should always be on his own side of the puck.

This is 1896 AAHL Rule 9, but changing the reference to "off-side" to "out of play", and stating that a player "should" always be on his own side of the puck, rather than the previous "must."

Rule 8: The puck may be stopped, but not carried not knocked on, by any part of the body, nor shall any player close his hand on or carry the puck to the ice in his hand. No player shall raise his stick above the shoulder, except in lifting the puck. Charging from behind, tripping, collaring, kicking or shinning shall not be allowed, and for any infringement of these rules, the referee may rule the offending player off the ice for that match, or for such portion of actual playing time as he may see fit.

The AAHL code once again reverts to Montreal rules where it before used an OHA rule, replacing the previous AHAC/OHA conglomeration that used to make up this rule. This is 1899 CAHL Rule 9.

Rule 9: In the event of any off-side play, puck, foul or puck out of bounds, within five (5) yards of the goal line, the puck shall in all cases be faced on the five (5) yard line, at a point at right angles to the goal line, opposite the spot where the foul, off-side play, or out of bounds occurred. Except, when such foul, off-side, or out of bounds occurs within three (3) yards of the side of the rink, in which case the puck shall be faced on the five (5) yard line at a point (3) yards from the side of the rink.

This rule is entirely re-written from its previous version, and the new version is not drawn from any other source. The interesting point is the reference to a "five-yard line", suggesting that there was a line placed on the ice to mark where faces were to take place, something other hockey leagues at the time did not have.

Rule 10: The goal-keeper must not during play, lie, kneel or sit upon the ice, but must maintain a standing position.

This is 1896 AAHL Rule 12, unchanged.

Rule 11: A goal shall be scored when the puck shall have passed between the goal posts from in front.

This is 1896 AAHL Rule 13, however it removes the reference to an imaginary line across the top of the posts. The reason for this becomes obvious when we get to Rule 19.

Rule 12: Hockey sticks shall not be more than three inches wide at any point.

Once again the code reverts to the Montreal version of a rule, whereas 1896 AAHL Rule 14 had been original to New York. This is 1899 CAHL Rule 13.

Rule 13: The puck must be made of vulcanized rubber, one inch thick all through and three inches in diameter.

This is 1896 AAHL Rule 15, unchanged.

Rule 14: The captains of the contesting teams shall agree upon a referee and two umpires (one to be stationed behind each goal), which positions shall not be changed during a match, and two time-keepers. In the event of the captains failing to agree on umpires and timekeepers the referee shall appoint same.

This is based on 1896 AAHL Rule 16, however there are now two timekeepers rather than one.

Rule 15: All disputes during the match shall be decided by the referee, and he shall have full control of all players and officials from the commencement to finish of matches, inclusive of stops, and his decision shall be final.

This is a reworded version of AAHL Rule 17.

Rule 16: All questions as to games shall be settled by the umpires, and their decisions shall be final.

This is AAHL Rule 18, the only revision being "goals" changed to "games".

Rule 17: In the event of any dispute as to the decision of an umpire or timekeeper, the referee shall have the power to remove and replace him.

This is a new rule, giving the referee the right to remove the goal umpires or timekeepers.

Rule 18: Any player guilty of using profane or abusive language to any officials or other players shall be liable to be ruled off by the referee, as per [Rule 8].

This is 1899 CAHL Rule 19.

Rule 19: A goal net shall be used.

This is a new rule, and explains why Rule 11 does not make reference to an imaginary line across the top of goalposts. The AAHL rules are therefore the first code to make reference to the use of goal nets.

1904 AAHL RULES

The AAHL amended its rules before the 1903/04 season, but made only one change, to Rule 9, with all other rules being identical to the previous code.

Source: Farrell, Arthur (1904). Spalding's Athletic Library Ice Hockey and Ice Polo Guide. New York: American Sports Publishing Company.

Rule 1: A team shall be composed of seven players, who shall be bona-fide members of the club they represent. No player shall be allowed to play on more than one team in the same series during a season.

Rule 2: The game shall be commenced and renewed by a face in the centre of the rink. Rink shall be at least 112 feet by 58 feet.

Goals shall be 6 feet wide and 4 feet high.

The puck shall be faced by being placed between the stick of two opponents, and the Referee then calling "play".

The goals shall be placed at least ten feet form the edge of the ice.

Rule 3: Two 20-minute halves, with an intermission of ten minutes between, will be the time allowed for matches, but no stops of more than five (5) minutes will be allowed. A match will be decided by the team winning the greatest number of games during that time. In case of a tie after playing the specified two 20-minutes halves, play will continue until one side secures a game, unless otherwise agreed upon between the captains before the match. Goals shall be changed after each half.

Rule 4: No change of players shall be made after a game has commenced, except for reasons of accidents or injury during the game.

Rule 5: Should any player be injured during the first half of a match and compelled to leave the ice, his side shall be allowed to put on a

137

spare man from the reserve to equalize the teams; should any player be injured during the second half of the match, the captain of the opposing team shall have the option of dropping a player to equalize the teams or allow his opponents to put on a man from the reserve. In the event of any dispute between the captains as to the injured player's fitness to continue the game, the matter shall at once be decided by the Referee.

Rule 6: Should the game be temporarily stopped by the infringement of any of the rules, the captain of the opposite team may claim that the puck be taken back and a face take place where it was last played from before such infringement occurred.

Rule 7: When a player hits the puck, anyone of the same side, who at such moment of hitting is nearer the opponent's goal is out of play, and may not touch the puck himself or in any way whatever prevent any other player from doing so until the puck has been played. A player should always be on his own side of the puck.

Rule 8: The puck may be stopped, but not carried not knocked on, by any part of the body, nor shall any player close his hand on or carry the puck to the ice in his hand. No player shall raise his stick above the shoulder, except in lifting the puck. Charging from behind, tripping, collaring, kicking or shinning shall not be allowed, and for any infringement of these rules, the referee may rule the offending player off the ice for that match, or for such portion of actual playing time as he may see fit.

Rule 9: When the puck goes off the ice or a foul occurs behind the goals, it shall be taken by the referee to five yards at right angles from the goal line and there faced. When the puck goes off at the sides, it shall be taken by the referee to five yards at right angles from the boundary line and there faced.

The oddly original 1901 AAHL Rule 9 is abandoned in favour of going back to the older Montreal version of this rule. This is 1904 CAHL Rule 10.

Rule 10: The goal-keeper must not during play, lie, kneel or sit upon the ice, but must maintain a standing position.

Rule 11: A goal shall be scored when the puck shall have passed between the goal posts from in front.

Rule 12: Hockey sticks shall not be more than three inches wide at any point.

Rule 13: The puck must be made of vulcanized rubber, one inch thick all through and three inches in diameter.

Rule 14: The captains of the contesting teams shall agree upon a referee and two umpires (one to be stationed behind each goal), which positions shall not be changed during a match, and two time-keepers. In the event of the captains failing to agree on umpires and timekeepers the referee shall appoint same.

Rule 15: All disputes during the match shall be decided by the referee, and he shall have full control of all players and officials from the commencement to finish of matches, inclusive of stops, and his decision shall be final.

Rule 16: All questions as to games shall be settled by the umpires, and their decisions shall be final.

Rule 17: In the event of any dispute as to the decision of an umpire or timekeeper, the referee shall have the power to remove and replace him.

Rule 18: Any player guilty of using profane or abusive language to any officials or other players shall be liable to be ruled off by the referee, as per [Rule 8].

Rule 19: A goal net shall be used.

The nine rules above are 1901 AAHL Rule 10 through Rule 19 respectively, all unchanged.

1909 AAHL RULES

Before the 1908/09 season, the code of laws of the AAHL underwent a significant rewriting. This was not based on any changes to any set of rules in Canada, though some of the changes were influenced by existing Canadian codes. It appears to be a deliberate attempt to reorganize and clarify the previous code, which had resulted from a gradual process of addition and change to the initial ruleset of 1877. Here, for the first time, a thorough revision was undertaken, rather than additions and modifications being made on an ad hoc basis.

For the most part, none of the changes affect how the game would be played on the ice. The offside rule is rewritten, but the effect is the same. Since the original 1877 code, from which other organized hockey codes were derived, was itself based on English field hockey laws, this appears to be the first code of rules for organized hockey that was essentially written from the ground up. This results in a much more cohesive code; the other contemporary codes seems disjointed and erratic in comparison.

In October 1909, the Intercollegiate Hockey League (made up of six of the eight colleges now known as the Ivy League: Columbia, Cornell, Dartmouth, Harvard, Princeton and Yale) adopted this code of rules verbatim.

Source: Toombs, Frederick R. (Ed.) (1909). Spalding's Athletic Library Office Ice Hockey Guide 1909. New York: American Sports Publishing Company.

Rule 1: The game of Hockey shall be played on ice by two teams, the players of which shall all be on skates. Its object shall be the lawful scoring of goals. The team scoring the greater number of goals during the playing period shall be declared the winner.

This new rule isn't really a rule, it's actually more of definition of the game of organized hockey. It contains a number of the factors used in the definition of organized hockey presented in Chapter One of this book.

Rule 2 (Rink): A hockey rink shall be at least 112 by 58 feet. The imaginary lines at the two ends of the rink shall be termed the goal lines. The two sides of the rink shall be known as the side lines.

The rink dimensions in this rule are from 1904 AAHL Rule 2, while the other bits are new.

Rule 3 (Goals): A goal shall be placed midway on each goal line, and shall consist of a goal net supported by two upright goal posts 4 feet in height, placed 6 feet apart, and at least 10 and not more than 15 feet from the edge of the ice. The goal posts must be firmly fixed to the ice.

Note – In the event of a goal post or net being broken or displaced, the referee shall at once stop the game and not allow play to be resumed until after the damage is repaired.

Most of this rule comes from 1893 AAHL Rule 3 rather than from a more recent version of the league's code. The placement of the goals has changed since 1893, however.

Rule 4 (Positions): There shall not be more than seven players on a hockey team. These players shall fill the position of goal, point, cover point and forwards, respectively. The goal position shall be the one that is directly in front of the goal. At no period during the play shall any player who fills this position, lie, kneel, or sit upon the ice. He must also always maintain a standing position. The point position is the one that is directly in front of the goal position. The cover point position is the one directly in front of the point position. The four forward positions shall be known as the left wing, the right wing, the center and the rover, respectively. The wing positions shall be at the two ends of the forward line. The center position is the one midway on the forward line, and it shall be the duty of the player who fills this position to face the puck. The rover position is between the cover point and the center position.

Note – It is to be understood that the positions herein named are the ones that the players are supposed to fill when the teams face off in the center of the ice.

This is a completely new rule, though it does include the existing prohibition against goaltenders falling to the ice to stop the puck. This is the first recorded rule that makes specific reference to positions other than goalkeeper.

While it states that the point plays directly in front of the goalkeeper, and the cover-point directly in front of the point, this was not the case in practice. Farrell (1899) states that the cover-point plays directly in line with the goaltender, but the point is off to one side. This provides the clear advantage of the point being able to better see the play as it develops. Presumably the side the point cheated toward would be based on the opposing centre's shot. A left-handed shooting centre will tend to go to his left, and so the point should play to the right of the goalkeeper. However, cheating to one side too much would be problematic, since a left-handed-shooting centre passes better to his right wing, so that side cannot be left open.

Rule 5 (Sticks): A hockey stick shall not be more than three inches wide at any part and not more than thirteen inches long at the blade. It shall be made entirely of wood. Tape binding is permissible, however. Each player shall carry a hockey stick in his hand, and shall be considered out of the play the moment he violates this rule.

This rule builds on 1904 AAHL Rule 12, and adds that a player is not permitted to play without a stick. If one has the stick knocked out of his hands, presumably the only thing he can legally do is retrieve it, without interfering with or assisting any other player when doing so.

Rule 6 (Skates): No player shall wear skates that are pointed or sharpened in such a manner as to be unnecessarily dangerous to other players. The referee shall by the judge, and shall refuse to allow a player to use such skates.

This new rules forbids the use of dangerous skates. It's unclear whether this is in response to an epidemic of dangerous skates, or if it was simply trying to anticipate potential problems in the future.

Rule 7 (Puck): A puck shall be made of vulcanized rubber one inch thick throughout. It shall be three inches in diameter, and shall weigh at least 7 6/16 and not more than 7 9/16 ounces.

This rule is largely from 1904 AAHL Rule 13, and adds particulars for the weight of the puck. Note that the puck described here is heavier than the modern NHL version, which is between 5 1/2 and 6 ounces in weight.

Rule 8 (Officials): There shall be a referee, an assistant referee, two goal umpires and two timekeepers for each match. Should a referee be unable to continue to officiate, his assistant shall become the referee. The referee shall fill all vacancies in other official positions that may occur during a match; or when the competing teams have been unable to agree; or when the selected officials are absent at the advertised starting hour. In the event of a dispute over the decision of an umpire, the referee may remove and replace the official.

Similar to 1904 AAHL Rule 14, this law sets out the officials for the game. The position of second (assistant) referee originated in the Eastern Canada Hockey Association, where it was sometimes referred to as the judge of play in practice.

Rule 9 (Duties of the Referee): The referee, before starting a match, shall see that the other officials are in their proper place. He shall see that the ice is in the condition for play and that the goals comply with the rules. The shall order the puck faced at the commencement of the game and at such other times as may be necessary. He shall have full control over the puck during the match. He shall call offside plays. He shall have the power to rule off for any period of the actual playing time that he may see fit any player who violates the rules. The referee shall, furthermore, perform all other duties that may be compulsory.

This new rule sets out the referee's duties in some detail, both before and during the match.

Rule 10 (Duties of the Assistant Referee): The assistant referee shall see that no player violates [Rule 19 – Foul Playing]. The shall have the power to rule off for any period of the actual playing time that he may see fit any player who violates said section. The assistant referee shall become the referee should the latter be unable to continue to officiate.

The assistant referee was introduced into the ECHA code of laws before the 1906/07 season, and the New Yorkers apparently seemed to think it was a good idea. Leaving all the officiating duties on the ice to one person is, after all, quite a lot of responsibility and things are bound to be missed.

Rule 11 (Duties of the Umpires): An umpire shall be stationed behind each goal. He shall inform the referee whenever the puck has passed between the goal posts from the front. He shall have no jurisdiction over the awarding of a goal. He shall stand upon the ice, and shall retain the same goal throughout the entire game.

Another rule that makes no changes to existing practice, this rule is interesting in that it notes the goal umpires cannot actually award goals, they simply inform the referee that the puck has entered the net. It's up to the referee to then determine whether the play was legal, and only then actually award a goal (see Rule 16).

Rule 12 (Duties of the Timekeepers): The timekeepers shall keep an accurate account of the time of the match, deducting time for stoppages in actual play. They shall immediately report to the referee any variance in time, and the referee shall decide the matter. The timekeepers shall keep an accurate account of penalties imposed, and no penalized player shall return to the ice without the permission of the timekeepers. The timekeepers shall be notified by the referee when a goal is scored, and shall keep an accurate record of the tallies. The final score shall be given by them to the referee at the close of the match. They shall, at half time, notify the contesting teams when five and when eight minutes have expired. They shall at half time, notify the referee when ten minutes have expired.

Similar to the 1909 ECHA rules, this is a detailed description of the timekeepers' duties, which now essentially include being official scorers as well.

Rule 13 (Length of Game): There shall be two halves of twenty minutes each, with an intermission of ten minutes between the two periods of play. At the end of the forty minutes' play, should the score be tied the teams shall change goals, and play shall be resumed at once and continued until a goal has been scored. Should the tie remain unbroken at the expiration of twenty minutes of extra play, the referee shall declare the game a draw. The referee must start each period on scheduled time.

1904 AAHL Rule 3 is changed to place a hard limit on the amount of overtime to be played.

Rule 14: Time shall be taken out whenever the game is suspended by the referees, and shall begin again when the puck is put in play. No delay of more than five minutes shall be allowed.

The 1904 AAHL code did not specify that the 40 minutes of game time was supposed to be stop-time, which is stated here.

Rule 15 (Substitutes): Substitutes shall be allowed only in the case of an injury. In the even of any dispute as to the injured player's ability continue, the matter shall at once be decided by the referee. Should any player be compelled to leave the game during the first half, his side shall be allowed a substitute. Should an injury occur during the balance of the game, the opposing team may either drop a man or allow a substitute in the place of the injured player. A player who has been replaced by a substitute shall not return to further participation in the game.

In exhibition or practice matches this rule may be altered by the captains.

The AAHL rules here are in line with the Canadian ECHA standard for the most part. It's unclear exactly why the option of dropping a player

145

only applies in the second half of the match. It's possible it is meant as a deterrent to gamesmanship in the second half, where the players will be more tired out and more likely to attempt to gain some extra rest via subterfuge.

Rule 16 (What Constitutes a Goal): A goal shall be scored when the puck shall have lawfully passed between the goal posts. No goal shall be allowed that is the direct and immediate result of loafing offside, an offside play, a kick or a throw by the hand. The referee shall decide upon these points, and may render his decision even after the puck has passed between the goal posts.

The usual description of a goal is expanded here to specify that goals scored by illegal means are not legal. It's a bit redundant, since each of the illegal ways of scoring a goal listed here are detailed elsewhere in the code (see Rule 18 and Rule 20).

Rule 17 (Face): A face shall consist of the referee placing the puck upon the ice on its largest surface between the sticks of two players, one from each team. The referee shall then order the play to begin. Should a player repeatedly refuse to lawfully face the puck, he shall be penalized by the referee. A face shall take place in the center of the ice at the beginning of each period and after the scoring of each goal. The referee may also order a face at any time and place he deems necessary. A face shall be in order whenever play is resumed.

This rule uses the OHA version of the faceoff definition, which specifies the orientation of the puck when it is placed on the ice. It also contains the first known reference to a delay of game penalty, for a player who repeatedly refuses to face the puck.

Rule 18 (Offside Play): Any player nearer to his opponent's goal line than is an imaginary line running through the center of the puck and parallel with the two goal lines is offside. A player offside shall be considered out of the play, and may not touch the puck himself or in any manner prevent any other player from doing so, until the puck has been touched by an opponent in any way whatsoever, or until it has been carried nearer than he is himself to the opponent's goal line. If a player violates this rule, the puck shall be faced where it was last played before the offside play occurred. In the event of the puck rebounding off the body of the player is the goal-keeper's position, the other players of his team shall be considered on side.

The AAHL code had, until now, simply used the Montreal version of the offside rule, using a word-for-word transcription. This new wording provides a third version of the offside rule (the Montreal and OHA versions being the others), however the effect of this wording is so similar to that of the Montreal version that it's difficult to understand the purpose of it.

There are conceivably situations where a player might have been considered onside under the Montreal rule, but would be offside under this rule, if it were not for the Montreal prescription that a player must always be on his own side of the puck.

More likely, this wording was intended to make the application of the rule easier on the referee, by keeping the focus on the puck at all times, rather than at the times when the puck is struck by a player. This rule defines what should be considered a player's "own side" of the puck: the area formed by his own goal line and a parallel imaginary line passing through the centre of the puck.

This wording makes it clearer that, so long as a pass recipient is never ahead of the puck, the puck can move forward on the ice and the play will still be onside. Art Farrell's 1899 comments about the best passes leading the pass recipient are borne out here.

Note that this rule, like the contemporary Montreal and OHA codes, considers a defensive player who plays a puck coming off the goaltender to be onside.

Rule 19 (Foul Playing): There shall be no unnecessary roughness. No player shall check another from behind. No player shall throw his stick. No player shall trip, hold with his hand or stick, kick, push or cross-check an opponent. No player shall interfere in any way with an opponent who is not playing the puck. No player shall raise his stick above his shoulder, except in lifting the puck. No player shall use profane or abusive language, or conduct himself in an unsportsmanlike manner. A player being out of the play shall not interfere with an opponent.

1904 AAHL Rule 8 lists a variety of prohibited actions, all of which have been carried forward from the original 1877 Montreal Rules: high-sticking, charging from behind, tripping, collaring, kicking and shinning. If we consider collaring a subset of holding, and shinning a subset of slashing, we see that all of these are still penalties today. The 1891 OHA rules also includes prohibitions against cross-checking and pushing, which are also both still penalties, the latter in the form of boarding.

But in the 32 years leading up to this rule, no recorded code of hockey laws included specific references to several common penalties we're used to in modern hockey. 1909 AAHL Rule 19 includes the first specific references to unnecessary roughness (roughing), holding with the hand or stick (holding and hooking respectively), interfering with a player who does not have the puck (interference) and conducting oneself in an unsportsmanlike manner (unsportsmanlike conduct).

These "new" penalties are almost certainly the codification of existing practice, and there are other recognized types of penalties at the time that may not be spelled out here. For example, in the 1911 New York Times *game reports for Intercollegiate Hockey League, there are a total of 28 penalties identified by type. 14 of these were for tripping.*

Two were holding, and two more for cross-checking. Four were for loafing offside, even though Rule 18 and Rule 19 do not spell out that a penalty can be given for such action. Finally, six of the penalties were for slashing. So even though it may not have yet been codified in the laws of the game, it was considered a penalty and was already known by the name we know it today.

Rule 20 (Puck Fouls): A player may stop the puck with any part of his stick or body. He may not, however, hold, bat, throw, kick or carry the puck with his skate or any part of his body. He may not close his hand upon the puck. The player in the goal position may catch the puck, but if he does he must at once drop the puck to the ice at his own feet.

This is the first part of 1904 AAHL Rule 8, with the additional provision that the goalkeeper is allowed to catch the puck with his hand. If he does so, however, he must immediately drop it straight down; no throwing it into the corner or to a teammate is allowed.

Rule 21 (When the Puck Leaves the Ice): When the puck goes off the ice or a foul occurs behind the goal line, it shall be brought out by the referee to a point five yards in front of the goal line, on a line at right angles thereto, from the point at which it left the ice or where the foul occurred, and there faced. In the aforementioned cases the puck shall always be based at least five yards to the left or the right of the nearer goal post. When the puck goes off the ice at the side lines it shall be taken by the referee to a point five yards out at right angles with the nearer side line and there faced.

The old puck-off-the-ice rule is essentially retained (1904 AAHL Rule 9), except that faces could no longer be taken in front of the goal; they had to be off to one side or the other.

Rule 22 (Penalties): In awarding a penalty the referee or his assistant shall use discretion in order that his ruling does not work against the better interests of the non-offending team

This is an explicit recognition that the offending team may have so offended in order to prevent a good scoring chance. It is similar in spirit to the modern rule that play is not whistled down on a penalty until the offending team has touched the puck.

149

1912 AAHL RULES

Before the 1911/12 season, the AAHL revised its code, adding the details of the duties of the penalty timekeepers, and overhauling that favourite target of early hockey law tinkering: the substitution rules.

Source: Toombs, Frederick R. (Ed.) (1912). Spalding's Athletic Library Office Ice Hockey Guide 1912. New York: American Sports Publishing Company.

Rule 1: The game of Hockey shall be played on ice by two teams, the players of which shall all be on skates. Its object shall be the lawful scoring of goals. The team scoring the greater number of goals during the playing period shall be declared the winner.

Rule 2 (Rink): A hockey rink shall be at least 112 by 58 feet. The imaginary lines at the two ends of the rink shall be termed the goal lines. The two sides of the rink shall be known as the side lines.

Rule 3 (Goals): A goal shall be placed midway on each goal line, and shall consist of a goal net supported by two upright goal posts 4 feet in height, placed 6 feet apart, and at least 10 and not more than 15 feet from the edge of the ice. The goal posts must be firmly fixed to the ice.

Note – In the event of a goal post or net being broken or displaced, the referee shall at once stop the game and not allow play to be resumed until after the damage is repaired.

Rule 4 (Positions): There shall not be more than seven players on a hockey team. These players shall fill the position of goal, point, cover point and forwards, respectively. The goal position shall be the one that is directly in front of the goal. At no period during the play shall any player who fills this position, lie, kneel, or sit upon the ice. He must also always maintain a standing position. The point position is the one that is directly in front of the goal position. The cover point position is the one directly in front of the point position. The four forward positions shall be known as the left wing, the right wing, the center and the rover,

150

respectively. The wing positions shall be at the two ends of the forward line. The center position is the one midway on the forward line, and it shall be the duty of the player who fills this position to face the puck. The rover position is between the cover point and the center position.

Note – It is to be understood that the positions herein named are the ones that the players are supposed to fill when the teams face off in the center of the ice.

Rule 5 (Sticks): A hockey stick shall not be more than three inches wide at any part and not more than thirteen inches long at the blade. It shall be made entirely of wood. Tape binding is permissible, however. Each player shall carry a hockey stick in his hand, and shall be considered out of the play the moment he violates this rule.

Rule 6 (Skates): No player shall wear skates that are pointed or sharpened in such a manner as to be unnecessarily dangerous to other players. The referee shall by the judge, and shall refuse to allow a player to use such skates.

Rule 7 (Puck): A puck shall be made of vulcanized rubber one inch thick throughout. It shall be thee inches in diameter, and shall weigh at least 7 6/16 and not more than 7 9/16 ounces.

Rule 8 (Officials): There shall be a referee, an assistant referee, two goal umpires and two timekeepers for each match. Should a referee be unable to continue to officiate, his assistant shall become the referee. The referee shall fill all vacancies in other official positions that may occur during a match; or when the competing teams have been unable to agree; or when the selected officials are absent at the advertised starting hour. In the event of a dispute over the decision of an umpire, the referee may remove and replace the official.

Rule 9 (Duties of the Referee): The referee, before starting a match, shall see that the other officials are in their proper place. He shall see that the ice is in the condition for play and that the goals comply with the rules. The shall order the puck faced at the commencement of the game and at such other times as may be necessary. He shall have full control over the puck during the match. He shall call offside plays. He shall have the power to rule off for any period of the actual playing time that he may see fit any player who violates the rules. The referee shall, furthermore, perform all other duties that may be compulsory.

Rule 10 (Duties of the Assistant Referee): The assistant referee shall see that no player violates [Rule 19 – Foul Playing]. He shall have the power to rule off for any period of the actual playing time that he may see fit any player who violates said section. The assistant referee shall become the referee should the latter be unable to continue to officiate.

Rule 11 (Duties of the Umpires): An umpire shall be stationed behind each goal. He shall inform the referee whenever the puck has passed between the goal posts from the front. He shall have no jurisdiction over the awarding of a goal. He shall stand upon the ice, and shall retain the same goal throughout the entire game.

Rule 12 (Duties of the Timekeepers): The timekeepers shall keep an accurate account of the time of the match, deducting time for stoppages in actual play. They shall immediately report to the referee any variance in time, and the referee shall decide the matter. The timekeepers shall be notified by the referee when a goal is scored, and shall keep an accurate record of the tallies. The final score shall be given by them to the referee at the close of the match. They shall, at half time, notify the contesting teams when five and when eight minutes have expired. They shall at half time, notify the referee when ten minutes have expired.

The above 12 rules are from 1909 AAHL Rule 1 through Rule 12 respectively, all unchanged.

Rule 13 (Duties of the Penalty Timekeepers): The penalty timekeepers shall keep an accurate account of penalties imposed, and no penalized player shall return to the ice without the permission of the penalty timekeepers. They shall also keep an accurate account of the time of any player who has been compelled to withdraw from the game and inform the referee when the said player is due again to report. They shall sit midway between the two goals, and shall be on the opposite side of the rink from the game timekeepers. They shall give an accurate report of all penalties imposed to the referee at the close of the match. All players penalized must sit with the penalty timekeepers.

Much of this new rule was cribbed from 1909 ECHA Rule 21, with some additional information on where the penalty timekeepers are to sit, and that penalized players are to sit with them, which is the first rule reference to something like a penalty box.

Rule 14 (Length of Game): There shall be two halves of twenty minutes each, with an intermission of ten minutes between the two periods of play. At the end of the forty minutes' play, should the score be tied the teams shall change goals, and play shall be resumed at once and continued until a goal has been scored. Should the tie remain unbroken at the expiration of twenty minutes of extra play, the referee shall declare the game a draw. The referee must start each period on scheduled time.

Rule 15: Time shall be taken out whenever the game is suspended by the referees, and shall begin again when the puck is put in play. No delay of more than five minutes shall be allowed.

The two above rules are 1909 AAHL Rule 13 and Rule 14 respectively, both unchanged.

Rule 16 A (Substitutes): Substitutes shall be allowed only in the case of an injury. The injured player's ability to continue shall at once be decided by the referee. Should the referee decide that the injured player cannot finish the game, the opposing side may either allow a substitute or drop a man to equalize the teams. Should the opposing side decide to allow a substitute and no substitute is ready, the opposing side must play its full team. Once the opposing side has allowed a substitute he may appear at any time during the balance of the game.

153

1909 AAHL Rule 15 has been altered so that there is always the option of allowing a substitute or dropping a man in the event of an opponent's injury, rather than this applying only in the second half. This rule as written presents a potential for abuse. If your opposition has brought only one spare player, for instance, and you manage to injure two of their players, you can play with a man advantage for the remainder of the match.

Rule 16 B (Substitutes): Should the referee decide that the injured player would be able to continue within seven minutes of actual not playing time, the opposing team must drop a man until that time has expired, or until the injured player returns to the game. Should the injured player be unable to continue at the expiration of seven minutes of actual and not playing time, the opposing side may either continue to drop a man or may allow a substitute. If no substitute is ready, the opposing side must play its full team. Once the opposing side has resumed its full strength, the other aggregation at any time thereafter may either play a substitute or the player who has been injured.

This new rules adds a previously-unknown level of complexity to the substitution-for-injured-player rules. Eventually, someone will have the brainstorm to simply allow unlimited substitutions, and such wrangling will no longer be necessary.

Rule 16 C (Substitutes): Should a player be compelled to leave the game for any reason other than injury, the opposing side must drop a man to equalize the teams. Should the player who has first left the ice be unable to continue at the expiration of seven minutes of actual and not playing time, the opposing side may either continue to drop a man or may allow a substitution. If no substitute is ready, the opposing side must play its full team. Once the opposing side has resumed its full strength, the other aggregation at any time thereafter may either play a substitute or the player who has first withdrawn from the game.

While 1909 AAHL Rule 15 stated that substitutes could only be played in case of injury, it did not actually specify the procedures for when a player cannot continue playing for another issue. Thus this new rule was needed.

Rule 16 D (Substitutes): All substitutes or other players entering or returning to the game must first report to the penalty timekeepers and then to the referee. They must obtain the permission of the referee before they resume play. This clause does not refer to players who have been penalized.

This new rule is an administrative matter with respect to substitute players entering the game.

Rule 16 E (Substitutes): Should it be necessary for the goalkeeper to retire from the game, play shall stop until the player is once more able to return to the contest. If at the end of seven minutes the goalkeeper is not able to resume play the match must go on with a substitute being allowed in the position. At any time during the seven minutes the team that has called for time may elect to play a substitute until the original goalkeeper is able to resume to contest.

This new rule makes reference to a team calling time. No provision has been made in any code of hockey laws to this date that describes how time can be called; presumably then it is left to the discretion of the referee.

Rule 16 F (Substitutes): A player other than the goalkeeper who has been replaced by a substitute cannot return to further participation in the game.

This new rule codifies the existing practice that a player who is replaced cannot return to the game.

Rule 16 G (Substitutes): In exhibition or practice matches this rule may be altered by the two captains.

This is the final part of 1909 AAHL Rule 15.

Rule 17 (What Constitutes a Goal): A goal shall be scored when the puck shall have lawfully passed between the goal posts. No goal shall be allowed that is the direct and immediate result of loafing offside, an offside play, a kick or a throw by the hand. The referee shall decide upon these points, and may render his decision even after the puck has passed between the goal posts.

Rule 18 (Face): A face shall consist of the referee placing the puck upon the ice on its largest surface between the sticks of two players, one from each team. The referee shall then order the play to begin. Should a player repeatedly refuse to lawfully face the puck, he shall be penalized by the referee. A face shall take place in the center of the ice at the beginning of each period and after the scoring of each goal. The referee may also order a face at any time and place he deems necessary. A face shall be in order whenever play is resumed.

Rule 19 (Offside Play): Any player nearer to his opponent's goal line than is an imaginary line running through the center of the puck and parallel with the two goal lines is offside. A player offside shall be considered out of the play, and may not touch the puck himself or in any manner prevent any other player from doing so, until the puck has been touched by an opponent in any way whatsoever, or until it has been carried nearer than he is himself to the opponent's goal line. If a player violates this rule, the puck shall be faced where it was last played before the offside play occurred. In the event of the puck rebounding off the body of the player is the goal-keeper's position, the other players of his team shall be considered on side.

Rule 20 (Foul Playing): There shall be no unnecessary roughness. No player shall check another from behind. No player shall throw his stick. No player shall trip, hold with his hand or stick, kick, push or cross-check an opponent. No player shall interfere in any way with an opponent who is not playing the puck. No player shall raise his stick above his shoulder, except in lifting the puck. No player shall use profane or abusive language, or conduct himself in an unsportsmanlike manner. A player being out of the play shall not interfere with an opponent.

Rule 21 (Puck Fouls): A player may stop the puck with any part of his stick or body. He may not, however, hold, bat, throw, kick or carry the puck with his skate or any part of his body. He may not close his hand upon the puck. The player in the goal position may catch the puck, but if he does he must at once drop the puck to the ice at his own feet.

Rule 22 (When the Puck Leaves the Ice): When the puck goes off the ice or a foul occurs behind the goal line, it shall be brought out by the referee to a point five yards in front of the goal line, on a line at right angles thereto, from the point at which it left the ice or where the foul occurred, and there faced. In the aforementioned cases the puck shall always be based at least five yards to the left or the right of the nearer goal post. When the puck goes off the ice at the side lines it shall be taken by the referee to a point five yards out at right angles with the nearer side line and there faced.

Rule 23 (Penalties): In awarding a penalty the referee or his assistance shall use discretion in order that his ruling does not work against the better interests of the non-offending team.

The above seven rules are from 1909 AAHL Rule 16 through Rule 22, all unchanged.

1915 AAHL RULES

There are few changes in the AAHL rules in this revision, and most of the changes that are there have to do with player substitutions. The constant tinkering that occurred with the substitution rules, in many leagues over many years, suggest that hockey officials were never convinced that their solutions were adequate. This would finally lead to unfettered substitutions, rendering these niggling details moot.

Source: Howard, Thomas A. (Ed.) (1917). Spalding's Athletic Library Official Ice Hockey Guide 1917. New York: American Sports Publishing Co.

Rule 1: The game of Hockey shall be played on ice by two teams, the players of which shall all be on skates. Its object shall be the lawful scoring of goals. The team scoring the greater number of goals during the playing period shall be declared the winner.

This is 1912 AAHL Rule 1, unchanged.

Rule 2 A (Rink): A hockey rink shall be at least 112 by 58 feet. The imaginary lines at the two ends of the rink shall be termed the goal lines. The two sides of the rink shall be known as the side lines. The ice surface bounded by the two side lines and the two goal lines shall be known as the field of play.

This is 1912 AAHL Rule 2, with the additional definition of what constitutes the "field of play."

Rule 2 B: There shall be an imaginary line twenty feet from each goal line and drawn inside the field of play. There shall also be an imaginary line at least ten and not more than twenty-five feet from each goal line and drawn outside of the field of play. These lines shall run parallel with the goal lines. They shall be known as zone lines and the ice surface between the two zone lines at each end of the rink shall be known as the goal zone. The intersection of the goal lines and the side lines, or the side lines extended, must be plainly marked in a manner that will last throughout the game. If possible, the zone lines shall also be marked on the ice.

This new rule defines the goal zone, the playing rules of which are covered in Rule 22.

Rule 2 C: The side lines, the side lines extended, and the zone lines outside the field of play shall be made of stationary material at least one foot in height.

This is another new rule, specifying how identifying lines are to be indicated on the ice.

Rule 3 (Goals): A goal shall be placed midway on each goal line, and shall consist of a goal net supported by two upright goal posts 4 feet in height, placed 6 feet apart. The goal posts must be firmly fixed to the ice.

Note – In the event of a goal post or net being broken or displaced, the referee shall at once stop the game and not allow play to be resumed until after the damage is repaired.

This is 1912 AAHL Rule 3, but without the specification of how far the goals are to be from the ends.

Rule 4 (Positions): There shall not be more than seven players on a hockey team. These players shall fill the position of goal, point, cover point and forwards, respectively. The goal position shall be the one that is directly in front of the goal. At no period during the play shall any player who fills this position, lie, kneel, or sit upon the ice. He must also always maintain a standing position. He cannot stop the puck by placing his stick horizontally on the ice. The point position is the one that is directly in front of the goal position. The cover point position is the one directly in front of the point position. The four forward positions shall be known as the left wing, the right wing, the center and the rover, respectively. The wing positions shall be at the two ends of the forward line. The center position is the one midway on the forward line, and it shall be the duty of the player who fills this position to face the puck. The rover position is between the cover point and the center position.

Note – It is to be understood that the positions herein named are the ones that the players are supposed to fill when the teams face off in the center of the ice.

To 1912 AAHL Rule 4 is added the restriction that a goaltender cannot stop the puck by laying his stick flat on the ice.

Rule 5 (Sticks): A hockey stick shall not be more than three inches wide at any part and not more than thirteen inches long at the blade. It shall be made entirely of wood. Tape binding is permissible, however. Each player shall carry a hockey stick in his hand, and shall be considered out of the play the moment he violates this rule.

Rule 6 (Skates): No player shall wear skates that are pointed or sharpened in such a manner as to be unnecessarily dangerous to other players. The referee shall by the judge, and shall refuse to allow a player to use such skates.

Rule 7 (Puck): A puck shall be made of vulcanized rubber one inch thick throughout. It shall be thee inches in diameter, and shall weigh at least 7 6/16 and not more than 7 9/16 ounces.

Rule 8 (Officials): There shall be a referee, an assistant referee, two goal umpires and two timekeepers for each match. Should a referee be unable to continue to officiate, his assistant shall become the referee. The referee shall fill all vacancies in other official positions that may occur during a match; or when the competing teams have been unable to agree; or when the selected officials are absent at the advertised starting hour. In the event of a dispute over the decision of an umpire, the referee may remove and replace the official.

Rule 9 (Duties of the Referee): The referee, before starting a match, shall see that the other officials are in their proper places. He shall see that the ice is in the condition for play and that the goals comply with the rules. The shall order the puck faced at the commencement of the game and at such other times as may be necessary. He shall have full control over the puck during the match. He shall call offside plays. He shall have the power to rule off for any period of the actual playing time that he may see fit any player who violates the rules. The referee shall, furthermore, perform all other duties that may be compulsory.

The five rules above are 1912 AAHL Rule 5 through Rule 8 respectively, all unchanged.

Rule 10 (Duties of the Assistant Referee): The assistant referee shall see that no player violates [Rule 20, 21 and 22]. He shall have the power to rule off for any period of the actual playing time that he may see fit any player who violates said section. The assistant referee shall become the referee should the latter be unable to continue to officiate.

Note - In the refereeing of games, it is advised that the referee and his assistant divide the field of play in half and each take one end thereof. When the puck is in the territory of the referee, he alone shall call offside plays, his assistant helping him according to the laws of hockey. When the puck passes the center of the ice into the territory of the assistant referee, that official shall assume the duties of the referee and he alone shall call offside plays, the referee helping as the assistant referee. In this manner, neither official shall be required to skate more than one-half of the playing surface. Changing in this manner does not affect the proper standing of either official. The referee shall remain the referee throughout the entire game and shall at all times assume all duties imposed upon him by [Rule 9] with the exception of calling offside play and the facing of the puck when the play is in the territory of the assistant referee.

The assistant referee is given additional responsibility in conjunction to the greater complexity of the code in Rule 20, Rule 21 and Rule 22. The suggestion provided in the note is an eminently reasonable one, that the two officials monitor one-half of the rink each, acting as referee when the play is in their own end, and as assistant referee when the play is in the other end.

Rule 11 (Duties of the Umpires): An umpire shall be stationed behind each goal. He shall inform the referee whenever the puck has passed between the goal posts from the front. He shall have no jurisdiction over the awarding of a goal. He shall stand upon the ice, and shall retain the same goal throughout the entire game.

This is 1912 AAHL Rule 11, unchanged.

Rule 12 (Duties of the Game Timekeepers): The game timekeepers shall keep an accurate account of the time of the match, deducting time for stoppages in actual play.

They shall immediately report to the referee any variance in time, and the referee shall decide the matter.

The timekeepers shall be notified by the referee when a goal is scored, and shall keep an accurate record of the tallies. The final score shall be given by them to the referee at the close of the match. They shall, at half time, notify the contesting teams when nine and when twelve minutes have expired. They shall at half time notify the referee when fifteen minutes have expired. They shall only tell the expired and unexpired time to the referee.

There are only minor adjustments to 1912 AAHL Rule 12 here, having to do with when the game timekeepers must notify the teams and referee when certain amounts of time have expired.

Rule 13 (Duties of the Penalty Timekeepers): The penalty timekeepers shall keep an accurate account of penalties imposed, and no penalized player shall return to the ice without the permission of the penalty timekeepers. They shall also keep an accurate account of the time of any player who has been compelled to withdraw from the game and inform the referee when the said player is due again to report. They shall sit midway between the two goals, and shall be on the opposite side of the rink from the game timekeepers. They shall give an accurate report of all penalties imposed to the referee at the close of the match. All players penalized must sit with the penalty timekeepers.

This is 1912 AAHL Rule 13, unchanged.

Rule 14 (Length of Game): There shall be two halves of twenty minutes each, with an intermission of fifteen minutes between the two periods of play. At the end of the forty minutes' play, should the score be tied the teams shall change goals, and play shall be resumed at once and continued until a goal has been scored. Should the tie remain unbroken at the expiration of twenty minutes of extra play, the referee shall declare the game a draw. The referee must start each period on scheduled time. Should either team be off the ice at the proper starting time of the second period, that team shall play with one man short for as many minutes as it has been late. The captain of the offending team shall decide which member of his team shall be dropped. This penalty shall be imposed in addition to any other that may be, or may have been, inflicted. The referee may inflict the same punishment upon any team that fails to appear at the scheduled starting our of a game.

1912 AAHL Rule 14 is amended here, changing the duration of intermission from 10 minutes to 15. The referee is also given the authority to award a man-advantage situation when one team holds up the game from its appointed starting time, with the genuinely clever idea of making the offending team short-handed for a number of minutes equal to the time is was late.

Rule 15: Time shall be taken out whenever the game is suspended by either referee, and shall begin again when the puck is put in play.

This is 1912 AAHL Rule 15, but without the provision that delays can last no longer than five minutes.

Rule 16 A (Substitutes): Substitutes shall be allowed only in the case of an injury. The injured player's ability to continue shall at once be decided by the referee. Should the referee decide that the injured player cannot finish the game, the opposing side may either allow a substitute or drop a man to equalize the teams. Should the opposing side decide to allow a substitute and no substitute is ready, the opposing side must play its full team. Once the opposing side has allowed a substitute he may appear at any time during the balance of the game.

Rule 16 B (Substitutes): Should the referee decide that the injured player would be able to continue within seven minutes of actual not playing time, the opposing team must drop a man until that time has expired, or until the injured player returns to the game. Should the injured player be unable to continue at the expiration of seven minutes of actual and not playing time, the opposing side may either continue to drop a man or may allow a substitute. If no substitute is ready, the opposing side must play its full team. Once the opposing side has resumed its full strength, the other aggregation at any time thereafter may either play a substitute or the player who has been injured.

Rule 16 C (Substitutes): Should a player be compelled to leave the game for any reason other than injury, the opposing side must drop a man to equalize the teams. Should the player who has first left the ice be unable to continue at the expiration of seven minutes of actual and not playing time, the opposing side may either continue to drop a man or may allow a substitution. If no substitute is ready, the opposing side must play its full team. Once the opposing side has resumed its full strength, the other aggregation at any time thereafter may either play a substitute or the player who has first withdrawn from the game.

Rule 16 D (Substitutes): All substitutes or other players entering or returning to the game must first report to the penalty timekeepers and then to the referee. They must obtain the permission of the referee before they resume play. This clause does not refer to players who have been penalized.

Rule 16 E (Substitutes): Should it be necessary for the goalkeeper to retire from the game, play shall stop until the player is once more able to return to the contest. If at the end of seven minutes the goalkeeper is not able to resume play the match must go on with a substitute being allowed in the position. At any time during the seven minutes the team that has called for time may elect to play a substitute until the original goalkeeper is able to resume to contest.

Rule 16 F (Substitutes): A player other than the goalkeeper who has been replaced by a substitute cannot return to further participation in the game.

Rule 16 G (Substitutes): In exhibition or practice matches this rule may be altered by the two captains.

Rule 17 (What Constitutes a Goal): A goal shall be scored when the puck shall have lawfully passed between the goal posts. No goal shall be allowed that is the direct and immediate result of loafing offside, an offside play, a kick or a throw by the hand. The referee shall decide upon these points, and may render his decision even after the puck has passed between the goal posts.

Rule 18 (Face): A face shall consist of the referee placing the puck upon the ice on its largest surface between the sticks of two players, one from each team. The referee shall then order the play to begin. Should a player repeatedly refuse to lawfully face the puck, he shall be penalized by the referee. A face shall take place in the center of the ice at the beginning of each period and after the scoring of each goal. The referee may also order a face at any time and place he deems necessary. A face shall be in order whenever play is resumed.

Rule 19 (Offside Play): Any player nearer to his opponent's goal line than is an imaginary line running through the center of the puck and parallel with the two goal lines is offside. A player offside shall be considered out of the play, and may not touch the puck himself or in any manner prevent any other player from doing so, until the puck has been touched by an opponent in any way whatsoever, or until it has been carried nearer than he is himself to the opponent's goal line. If a player violates this rule, the puck shall be faced where it was last played before the offside play occurred. In the event of the puck rebounding off the body of the player is the goal-keeper's position, the other players of his team shall be considered onside.

The ten rules above are 1912 AAHL Rule 10 through Rule 19 respectively, all unchanged.

Rule 20 (Loafing Offside): No player shall loaf offside. A player is loafing offside when, in the opinion of the referee or his assistant, he is not making a bona fide attempt to get or remain onside.

Loafing offside was always prohibited in the AAHL rules, even if it has not previously been codified in this manner. This also gives us an idea as to the definition of loafing offside, which is exactly as you would expect it to be.

Rule 21 (Foul Playing): There shall be no unnecessary roughness. No player shall check another from behind. No player shall violently check another against the boards. No player shall throw his stick. No player shall trip, hold with his hand or stick, kick, push or cross-check an opponent. No player shall interfere in any way with an opponent who is not playing the puck. A player is playing the puck within the meaning of these laws when he has the puck within the control of his stick. No player shall raise his stick above his shoulder, except in lifting the puck. No player shall use profane or abusive language, or conduct himself in an unsportsmanlike manner. A player being out of the play shall not interfere with an opponent.

To 1912 AAHL Rule 20 is added the provision that violent checking into boards is prohibited, and a definition of when a player is considered to be playing the puck for purposes of interference. This has a narrower meaning that it does today; it actually requires the player to be in control of the puck.

Rule 22 (Playing in the Goal Zone): A player on the defending side who is within his own goal zone shall not be considered as loafing offside. A player on the defending side may cover up an opponent while in the goal zone. However, he may not check the stick or interfere with the movements of an opponent until the latter attempts to play the puck. A player on the defending side while within his own goal zone may play any puck passed or shot by an opponent without being considered offside. Should it be necessary to face the puck in a goal zone, all players must be onside. A player shall be considered on the defending side when the puck is in the goal zone of the goal that he is defending.

Note 1 - A player on the defending side, who is skating outside of his own goal zone, when the puck is within that zone, shall be considered as loafing offside and shall at once make every effort to enter his own goal zone.

Note 2 - A player on the defending side, while is his own goal zone when a puck is shot or passed by an opponent who is within the goal zone, may legally take possession of the puck either in the goal zone or in the field of play.

This new rule spells out what defending players are allowed to do in their own end. The most important is that the loafing offside rule does not apply; defending players are not all required to attempt to get back behind the puck as the opponents bear down on the goal.

Rule 23 (Puck Fouls): A player may stop the puck with any part of his stick or body. He may not, however, hold, bat, throw, kick or carry the puck with his skate or any part of his body. He may not close his hand upon the puck. The player in the goal position may catch the puck, but if he does he must at once drop the puck to the ice at his own feet.

Rule 24 (When the Puck Leaves the Ice): When the puck goes off the ice or a foul occurs behind the goal line, it shall be brought out by the referee to a point five yards in front of the goal line, on a line at right angles thereto, from the point at which it left the ice or where the foul occurred, and there faced. In the aforementioned cases the puck shall always be based at least five yards to the left or the right of the nearer goal post. When the puck goes off the ice at the side lines it shall be taken by the referee to a point five yards out at right angles with the nearer side line and there faced.

Rule 25 (Penalties): In awarding a penalty the referee or his assistance shall use discretion in order that his ruling does not work against the better interests of the non-offending team.

The three rules above are 1912 AAHL Rule 21 through Rule 23 respectively, all unchanged.

PCHA Rules

In 1911, star hockey players Lester and Frank Patrick invested their father's lumber money into the creation of a major professional hockey league in British Columbia, called the Pacific Coast Hockey Association (PCHA). The warmer weather of Canada's West Coast necessitated the building of the country's first artificial ice rinks to house the three teams. The Patricks by no means stopped there in terms of innovation. Boileau and Wolf (2000) credit the PCHA's bosses with many changes to the game that have lasted to the present day:

"From the PCHA emerged such ideas as allowing the forward pass, installing numbers on players' sweaters, allowing goaltenders to leave their feet to make saves, the introduction of the blue lines and the goal crease, the awarding of assists, delayed penalties and the penalty shot."

It may be worth noting that while the 1911 NHA Rules specify that players are to wear numbers on their sweaters, the 1911 PCHA Rules have no such provision.

The blue lines and the forward pass are intimately related, since as Craig Bowlsby discusses in his book *1913: The Year They Invented the Future of Hockey*, at first the offside rules were only suspended in what is now called the neutral zone. In later years forward passing became permissible in the defensive zone, and finally in the offensive zone as well, but by this time the PCHA had ceased to exist, being absorbed into the Western Hockey League, which in turn was bought out by the NHL in 1926.

But all of this was yet to come when the PCHA began play in the 1911/12 hockey season, using the code of laws printed below. The degree of similarity between this code and the 1911 NHA rules is noteworthy; the PCHA version leaves off the last few NHA rules, and uses an older version of the penalty rules, but overall it's clear that either one code was based on the other, or both codes were developed in conjunction with each other.

Based on the analysis below, it seems most likely that the PCHA rule-makers took the 1911 NHA rules as its basis, but undid certain changes made by the eastern league that season back to their previous versions, for instance keeping the old composition of team rule, and the old penalty rules.

1911 PCHA RULES

Source: Pacific Coast Hockey Association, Victoria Arena Rick, Official Scorebook Season 1912.

Rule 1 (Composition of Team): A team shall be composed of seven players, who shall be bona fide members of the clubs they represent.

This is 1909 ECHA Rule 1, but with no restriction on player movement from club to club.

Rule 2 (Commencement of Game and Definition of a Face): The game shall be commenced and renewed by a face in the centre of the rink.

The home club shall have the privilege of choosing the goals to defend at the start of the game.

The puck shall be faced by being placed on the ice between the sticks of two opponents and the referee giving the signal to play.

Rule 3 (Time of Match and How Won): Three 20 minutes with an intermission of 10 minutes between, will be the time allowed for the matches. A match will be decided by the team winning the greatest number of games during that time. In case of a tie after playing the specified 60 minutes, play will continue until one side secures a game, unless otherwise agreed between the captains before the match. It being understood, however, that any extra time played shall be considered part of the match. Goals shall be changed after each 20 minutes.

Rule 4 (Change of Players): Players may be changed at any time by the Captain of the club after having notified the referee, and said substitute shall be placed on the ice and the original player removed, without interruption. It being understood, how understood however [sic], that once a player is removed from the ice, he is not at liberty to return again during that match.

Rule 5: In the event of a player being injured or compelled to leave the ice during a match, he may retire from the game for the period of 10 minutes playing time but must be continued immediately without the teams leaving the ice, the opposing team dropping a player to equalize with the exception to a goalkeeper, who will be allowed 10 minutes to recuperate. If at the expiration of 10 minutes the injured player is unable to resume his position on the ice, his Captain may put on a substitute, providing the injury occurred before the termination of the second period. If, however, the player was injured during the third period, the opposing Captain shall have the option of dropping a man for the balance of the playing time or allowing the injured side to put on a substitute. The man dropped to equalize shall return to the ice when the injured player does or when a substitute is put on. An injured player may not resume play after his place has been filled by a substitute, without the consent of the opposing team's Captain.

Rule 6 (Face of Puck After Foul Has Been Committed): Should the game be temporarily stopped by the infringement of any of the rules, the Captain of the team not at fault may claim that the puck be taken back and faced where it was last played from before such infringement occurred.

Rule 7 (Offside Play): When a player hits the puck, any one of the same side, who at such moment of hitting is nearer the opponent's goal line it out of play, and may not touch the puck himself or in any way whatever prevent another player from doing so, until the puck has been played. A player should always be on his own side of the puck. In the event of the puck rebounding off goal-keeper's body, players of his team touching puck to be considered onside.

The above six rules are most likely identical to 1911 NHA Rules 2, 3, 4, 5, 6 and 8 respectively. These rules likely reflect the actual NHA wording, which is unconfirmed at this time.

Rule 8 (Foul Play): The puck may be stopped, but not carried or knocked on by any part of the body, not shall any player close his hand on, or carry the puck to the ice in his hand. No player shall raise his stick above the shoulder except in lifting the puck. Charging from behind, tripping, collaring, kicking, or shinning shall not be allowed, and for infringement of these rules the referee or his assistant may rule the offending player off the ice for that match, or for such portion of actual playing time as he may see fit, but it shall not be necessary to stop the game to enforce this rule.

This is 1909 ECHA Rule 8. While the 1911 NHA rules were more refined in the sense of the details of what constituted penalties and the seriousness of different infringements, its focus on fines instead of penalties was, in my opinion, contrary to the best interests of the game on the ice. So the Patricks' apparent decision to stick with the old way in this regard made a great deal of sense.

Rule 9 (Face of Puck After Being Out of Bounds): When the puck does off the ice or a foul occurs behind the goals, it shall be taken by the referee to five yards at right angles from the boundary line, and there faced.

Rule 10 (Goal Keeper): The goal keeper must not, during play, kneel or sit upon the ice, but must maintain a standing position.

Rule 11 (How Goal Scored): A goal shall be scored when the puck shall have passed between the goal posts from in front, and below an imaginary line across the top of the posts.

Rule 12 (Dimensions of Stick): Hockey sticks shall not be more than three inches wide at any part.

Rule 13 (Dimensions of Puck): The puck must be made of vulcanized rubber, one inch thick all through and three inches in diameter.

The above five rules are most likely identical to 1911 NHA Rules 7, 12, 11, 13 and 14 respectively. These rules likely reflect the actual NHA wording, which is unconfirmed at this time.

Rule 14 (Appointment of Umpires and Timekeepers): The Captains of the competing teams shall agree upon two time-keepers, one penalty time-keeper, two umpires (one to be stationed behind each goal, which position shall not be changed during a match). In the event of the Captains failing to agree upon umpires and time-keepers, the referee shall appoint them.

This is 1909 ECHA Rule 14, unchanged. It includes a reference to an assistant referee, though such an official is not mentioned elsewhere in the rules. The method for appointing the referee is not specified either, so it's quite possible that an assistant referee was used.

Rule 15 (Disputes): All disputes during a match shall be decided by the referee.

This is most likely identical to 1911 NHA Rule 16. The rule likely reflects the actual NHA wording, which is unconfirmed at this time.

Rule 16 (Umpire's Decision Final): All questions as to game shall be settled by the umpires, and their decisions shall be final.

This is 1909 ECHA Rule 16, unchanged.

Appendix II

NOTABLE NON-CONNECTIONS

There are some other notable sports that may be seen as having some connection or relevance to the discussion of the origin of the rules of organized hockey. They are each briefly discussed below.

BANDY

Bandy is a sport closely related to organized hockey. Using the definition of organized hockey we arrived at in Chapter One, the only truly notable difference between that game and modern bandy is that the former uses a puck while the latter uses a ball. The first published rules for bandy were in the 1882 book *Handbook of Fen Skating*, by the Bury Fen skating club, which was located in East Anglia, near some oft-flooded meadows that made for good skating. Referred to in that book as hockey on the ice, but noted that it is "the counterpart to bandy on *terra firma*, the method of the two games being substantially the same" and this is now seen as the beginning of the version of bandy that developed into the modern game.

This book refers to bandy as a field game, and if we examine the rules as reproduced below, we can see that it has some similarities with the rules of field hockey we have discussed earlier. Although the field hockey codes presented earlier in this book predate the bandy rules, it is unlikely that the latter developed from the former. Much more likely is that they represent two separate evolutions of a field stick-ball game. Bury is in the East of England, while the Hockey Association rules developed in the London area, so it was most likely parallel development. As such these rules are not directly relevant to the history of organized hockey rules, but are interesting nonetheless and are therefore reproduced here.

Bury Fen Bandy Rules – 1882
Source: Goodman, Neville and Albert Goodman (1882). Handbook of Fen Skating. London: Sampson Low

174

Rule 1: The game is commenced by one player taking the ball and standing in the centre of the field; the others grouping themselves at their discretion. The holder of the ball then throws it straight up into the air, and when it falls it becomes general property.

Rule 2: During the play the ball may not be taken in the hand, but may be stopped and struck by any part of the body and skate or bandy.

Rule 3: If the ball is knocked off the ice on either side or over that line which is considered the boundary, it may be picked up by the first comer who must take it back as near as possible to the place where it left the field, or where it crossed the boundary, (as this gives rise to disputes, the rule is sometimes altered so that the ball has to be thrown or placed opposite the point at which it comes to rest). The player having the ball in hand may choose his own time and may either have a free hit or may throw it anywhere in a line across the field, but not obliquely.

Rule 4: If the ball is knocked behind the goal line it is "a bye," and one of the owners of that goal has a free knock off from any point either behind the goal or within six yards in front of it.

Rule 5: If the ball is knocked through the goal "the goal is made," and the winning side take that goal instead of their own and the game is started again, as already described, by another throw up in the centre.

Rule 6: If half the time for the match expires without a goal being made, play is stopped, and the side change goals and commence again by a throw-up in the centre.

Rule 7: The bandy must never be thrown out of the hand, nor may it be swung about with the intention of hitting or intimidating or of catching or tripping an opponent. Nevertheless, for the purpose of preventing the ball being hit at that particular moment, the bandy may be used to hit, catch, lift up or bear down the bandy of an opponent.

Rule 8: No intentional catching by the hand of any part of an opponent's body, clothes, or bandy is allowed.

Rule 9: No intentional running against an opponent, or intentional interposing of the body between him and the ball is allowed, nevertheless, the ball itself may be moved so that it is protected by the body. It is a well understood thing, that none of the opponents may stand in the goal or near it, so as to impede the goal keeper, nor should they stand immediately in front, when the ball is knocked off, so as to necessitate a block.

ROLLER POLO

Fitsell (2006) points out that when organized hockey was first played in Kingston, Ontario in 1886, the players borrowed sticks from a local roller polo club for the match. Organized roller polo had begun in New England in 1878, and subsequently spread throughout parts of the United States and Canada. Not only was roller polo a popular game, but it spawned a version played on ice, called ice polo. Since the origin of the differences between the OHA rules and Montreal rules is unknown, and since the first Kingston match used polo sticks, one might suppose that the rules of polo might have had some influence on the OHA code. However, if you read through the rules below, you see that any similarities in the codes are incidental, and there is no reason to suspect this had any significant influence on the development of organized hockey laws.

Official Revised (Roller Polo) Rules – 1885
Source: Henley, M.C. (1885). Henley's Official Polo Guide. Richmond, Ind: M. Cullaton & Co.

Rule 1: Each team shall consist of six players, to be designated as follows: On goal-tend; two half-backs; one cover-point; two rushers.

Rule 2: The ball shall be the regulation rubber-covered polo ball.

Rule 3: The sticks shall not exceed four feet in length, or one inch and one-eighth in diameter, or fifteen ounces in weight. The crook of the stick must be covered with leather, but no metallic substance will be allowed near that end of the stick.

Rule 4: The goal shall be the cage goal, three feet high and six feet long.

Rule 5: In playing a game the front of the cage must be not less than ten feet from the end, and equidistant from the sides of the playing surface of the rink.

Rule 6: No person shall play in a championship match who has played on any other team in this association, in a championship match, within thirty days previous to the match, and he must also have been a regular member of the team not less than fifteen days before said match, unless by consent, given in the presence of the referee, by the captains.

Rule 7: No player except the goal-tend shall be allowed within a semi-circle plainly indicated in front of the goal, the radius of which must be three feet from the center of the goals line, except at such times as the ball may be within said semi-circle.

Rule 8: There shall be an official referee, and also a time-keeper. No persons but the the players and referee shall be permitted on the surface during a match, unless assistance is to be rendered in case of accident, or unless upon mutual invitation of the captains and referee. The referee shall start and call the game, and settle all disputed points. If a championship match is prolonged, and neither side is adjudged a winner, he shall call the game and postpone the match to some definite time within thirty days.

Rule 9: There shall be a corps of official referees appointed by the Executive Committee. The expense of an official referee shall be paid by the manager of the rink in which the game is played. If an official referee fails to appear at any game, there shall be a referee appointed by the manager of the home rink, but said referee must not be connected in any way with said home rink.

Rule 10: The referee shall toss for the positions of the teams in presence of the captains, and the positions shall be reversed after each goal.

Rule 11: To start the game, the ball shall be placed in the middle of a straight line drawn through the center of each goal, and at the whistle of the referee shall be charged upon by a player from each team.

Rule 12: To constitute a championship match three out of five goals must be won by one of the competing teams, unless a different agreement be made by the captains, in presence of the referee, previous to the beginning of the match. Unless a goal be won meantime the referee shall call game at the end of each half hour. The rests between goals, or when play is called at the half hour limit shall not be over five minutes. If three out of five goals be the game played, if, at the final call of game by the referee, one team shall call of game by the referee, one team shall have won two goals to none for the other, the winners of the two goals shall be considered winners of the match. If there be a postponement by the referee, the match shall be renewed where it terminated, but the personnel of each team must be the same.

Rule 13: A goal is won by the passage of the ball into the cage, where it must remain until removed by the referee. If any player interfere with the ball when it is in the cage, or removes or attempt to remove the ball from the cage, the goal shall be given to the opposing side, and he shall be ordered from the floor by the referee, and no substitute allowed in his place.

Rule 14: If the ball go out of bounds the referee shall blow his whistle to call game, and place the ball at the point opposite where it went out, at least four feet from the rail. In re-commencing play, the player who do so must stand in position to knock the ball lengthwise of the surface, with their backs toward the sides.

Rule 15: Game shall be called by the referee whenever a foul occurs. Upon the renewal of the game the ball must be placed where the foul occurred.

Rule 16: It shall be deemed a foul: 1, if any player stop or strike the ball when any part of his person is touching the surface; 2, if any player catch or bat the ball with his hands or arms, though he is permitted to stop the ball with either his skates, hands, arms, or any part of his person; 3, if any player, save the goal-tend, who may do so, kick the ball with his foot or skate; 4, if any player intentionally violates Rule 7.

Rule 17: Any act by any player that is manifestly intended as an unwarrantable interference by one player with another, may be declared a foul by the referee, from his own observation, or upon complaint by the captain of the offended side.

Rule 18: Three fouls, other than when the ball leaves the bounds, made by either side, during the contest for a goal, shall constitute a goal for the opposing side.

178

Rule 19: If a dispute shall arise upon the surface, it shall be settled by the referee and the two captains. The players shall immediately resume their positions on the floor, and take no part in the discussion unless called upon by the referee.

Rule 20: If the referee decides that a foul in the goal by the goal-tend, or any player taking his place for the time being, it shall be adjudged as a goal for the opposite team.

Rule 21: If any club refuses to play a schedule game, or to abide by the decision of the referee, which, in all cases, shall be final, they shall forfeit the game, and be liable to expulsion from the league.

Rule 22: In case of an injury to any player a substitute may be appointed.

Rule 23: All games shall be played upon regular rink skates, without any extra appliances, and having plain revolving boxwood rollers, not less than one and three-quarter inches in diameter, and not exceeding one inch in width, and no others will be allowed.

Rule 24: The skates of each club shall be examined by the referee before the game commences. No player shall be allowed to leave the surface, except in the case of injury, without permission of the referee. When any player or his substitute returns to the floor his skates shall again undergo inspection by the referee.

Rule 25: In the event of any player using profane or obscene language upon the floor, or acting in any ungentlemanly manner, sufficient to attract the attention of the audience, he may be ordered from the surface by the referee, and no substitute shall be allowed in his place.

Rule 26: All championship games shall be commenced with a new regulation league ball, taken from a sealed box, bearing the signature of the Secretary of the League, by the referee of the game, in the presence of the audience. The winning team shall be the possessor of the ball.

RUGBY FOOTBALL

Association football was not the only onside version of football being played in England at the time the Hockey Association rules were

written. The first written rules of rugby football were published in 1845, and a significant revision was done in 1871. According to Bodleian Library (2010), the association football code was originally developed as a set of compromise rules, intended to allow boys from different schools, each with its own set of rules, to play football together. It was not intended to replace these codes but to supplement them, though it ultimately subsumed them. But Rugby School maintained its own rules, which became the game known as rugby today.

In order to demonstrate that association football was an influence on the Hockey Association code, while rugby was not, the complete 1871 laws of rugby football are presented below. Note the distinct lack of relevance to the first Montreal code, at least relative to association football.

Rules 22 through 25 below deal with the offside rules of rugby football. While certainly similar to the Hockey Association offside rule, it's very clear that the association football code is much more closely influential in the development of the former. However, it is interesting to note that while the rugby football rules did not influence the Montreal line of organized hockey rules, Rule 24 is actually very reminiscent of the OHA offside rule, at least with respect to the concept of skating a man onside, so this may be the source of the difference between the OHA and Montreal versions of the offside rules.

Rules of Rugby Football – 1871
Source: Bodleian Library (2010).

Rule 1: A drop kick or drop is made by letting the ball fall from the hands and kicking it at the very instant it rises.

Rule 2: A place kick or place is made by kicking the ball after it has been placed in a nick made in the ground for the purpose of keeping it at rest.

Rule 3: A punt is made by letting the ball fall from the hands and kicking it before it touches the ground.

Rule 4: Each goal shall be composed of two upright posts exceeding 11 foot in height from the ground and placed 18 ft 6 inches apart with a cross bar 10 feet from the ground.

Rule 5: A goal can only be obtained by kicking the ball from the Field of Play direct (i.e. without touching the dress or person of any player of either side) over the Cross bar of the opponents' goal whether it touch such Crossbar or posts or not: but if the ball goes directly it over either of the goal posts it is called a poster and is not a goal.

Rule 6: A goal may be obtained from any kind of kick except a punt.

Rule 7: A match shall be decided only by a majority of goals.

Rule 8: The ball is dead when it rests absolutely motionless on the ground.

Rule 9: A touch down is when a player putting his hand upon the ball on the ground in touch or in goal stops it so that it remains dead or fairly so.

Rule 10: A tackle is when the holder of the ball is held by one or more players of the opposite side.

Rule 11: A scrummage takes place when the holder of the ball being in the field of play puts it down on the ground in front of himself and all who have closed round on their respective sides endeavour to push their opponents back and by kicking the ball to drive it in the direction of the opposite goal line.

Rule 12: A player may take up the ball whenever it is rolling or bounding except in a scrummage.

Rule 13: It is not lawful to take up the Ball when dead (except in order to bring it out after it has been touched down in touch or in goal) for any purpose whatever - whenever the ball shall have been so unlawfully taken up it shall at once be brought back to where it was so taken up and there put down.

Rule 14: In a scrummage it is not lawful to touch the Ball with the hand under any circumstances whatever.

Rule 15: It is lawful for any player who has the ball to run with it, and if he does so it is called a run - if a player runs with the ball until he gets behind his opponents goal line and there touches it down, it is called a run in.

Rule 16: It is lawful to run in anywhere across the goal line.

Rule 17: The goal line is in goal and the touch-line is in touch.

Rule 18: In the event of any player holding or running with the ball being tackled and the ball being fairly held he must at once cry down and there put it down.

Rule 19: A maul in goal is when the holder of the Ball is tackled inside goal line or being tackled immediately outside is carried or pushed across it and he or the opposite side or both endeavour to touch the ball down. In all cases the ball when so touched down shall belong to the players of the side who first had possession just before the maul commenced unless the opposite side have gained entire possession of it.

Rule 20: In case of a maul in-goal those players only who are touching the ball with their hands when it crosses the goal line may continue in the maul in-goal and when a player has once released his hold of the Ball after it is inside the goal line he may not again join in the maul and if he attempts to do so may be dragged out by the opposite side. But if a player when running in is tackled inside the goal line then only the player who first tackled him or if two or more tackle him simultaneously they only may join in the maul.

Rule 21: Touch in-goal (see plan) Immediately the Ball whether in the hands of a player (except for the purpose of punt out see Rule 29) or not goes into touch in-goal it is at once dead and out of the game of and is brought out as provided by Rules 41 and 42.

Rule 22: Every player is on side but is put off side if he enters a scrummage from his opponents' side or being in a scrummage gets in front of the Ball, or when the ball has been kicked, touched or is being run with by any of his own side behind him (i.e. between himself and his own goal line).

Rule 23: Every player when offside is out of the game and shall not touch the ball in any case whatever, either in or out of touch or goal, or in any way interrupt or obstruct any player, until he is again on side.

Rule 24: A player being offside is put on side when the ball has been run five yards with or kicked by or has touched the dress or person of any player of the opposite side or when one of his own side has run in front of him.

Rule 25: When a player has the Ball none of his opponents who at the time are offside may commence or attempt to run, tackle or otherwise interrupt such player until he has run five yards.

Rule 26: Throwing back. It is lawful for any player who has the Ball to throw it back towards his own goal, or to pass it back to any player of his own side who is at the time behind him in accordance with the rules of on side.

Rule 27: Knocking on i.e. deliberately hitting the ball with the hand and Throwing Forward i.e. throwing the ball in the direction of the opponents' goal line are not lawful, as provided by the next rule the captain of the opposite side may require it to be brought back to the spot whence it was so knocked or thrown forward and there put down.

Rule 28: A Fair Catch is a catch made direct from a kick or a throw forward or Knock-on by one of the opponents' side, or from a punt out or a punt on (see Rules 29 and 30) provided the catcher makes a mark with his heel at the spot where he has made the catch and no other of his own side touch the ball (see Rules 43 & 44).

Rule 29: A punt out is a punt made after a touchdown by player from behind his opponents goal line and from touch in-goal if necessary towards his own side who must stand outside the goal line and endeavour to make a fair catch or to get the ball and run in or drop a goal (see 49 and 51).

Rule 30: A punt on is a punt made in a manner similar to a punt out and from touch if necessary by player who has made a fair catch from a punt out or another punt on.

Rule 31: If the ball goes into touch the first player on his side who touches it down must bring it to the spot where it crossed the touchline, or if a player when running with the ball cross or put any part of either foot across the touchline, he must return with the ball to the spot where the line the was so crossed, and from thence return it into the filed of play as provided by the following.

Rule 32: He must then himself or by one of his own side, either (i) bound it out in the field of play and then run with it kick it or throw it back to his own side or (ii) throw it out at right angles to the touchline or (iii) walk out with it at right angles to the touchline any distance not less than five or more than 15 yards and there put it down first declaring how far he intends to walk out.

Rule 33: If two or more players holding the ball are pushed into touch the ball shall belong in touch to the player who first had hold of it when in the field of play and has not yet released his hold of it.

Rule 34: If the ball when thrown out of touch be not thrown out at right angles to the touchline the captain of either side may at once claim to have it thrown out again.

Rule 35: A catch made when the ball is thrown out of touch is not a fair catch.

Rule 36: Kick-off is a place kick from the centre of the field of play and cannot count as a goal. The opposite side must stand at least 10 yards in front of the ball until it has been kicked.

Rule 37: The ball shall be kicked off (i) at the commencement of the game (ii) after a goal has been obtained.

Rule 38: The sides shall change goals as often as and whenever a goal is obtained unless it has been otherwise agreed by the captains before the commencement of the match.

Rule 39: The captains of the respective sides shall toss up before the commencement of the match, the winner of the toss shall have the option of goals or the kick-off.

Rule 40: Whenever a Goal shall have been obtained the side that has lost the goal shall then kick-off.

Rule 41: Kick out is a drop kick by one of the players of the side which has had to touch the ball down in their own goal or into whose touch in-goal the ball has gone (Rule 21) and is the mode of bringing the ball again into play, and cannot count as a goal.

Rule 42: Kick out must be a drop kick and from not more than 25 yards outside the kickers goal line. If the ball when kicked out pitch in touch it must be taken back and kicked out again. The kicker's side must be behind the ball when kicked out.

Rule 43: A player who has made and claimed a fair catch shall thereupon either take a drop kick or a punt or place the ball for a place kick.

Rule 44: After a fair catch has been made the opposite side may come up to the catcher's mark and (except in cases under rule 50) the catcher's side retiring the ball shall be kicked from such mark or from a spot any distance in a direct line (not being in touch) behind it.

Rule 45: A player may touch the ball down in his own goal at any time.

Rule 46: A side having touched the ball down in their opponents' goal, shall try at goal either by a place kick or a punt out.

Rule 47: If a try at goal be made by a place kick a player of the side who has touched the ball down shall bring it up to the goal line subject to rule 48 in a straight line from and opposite to the spot where the ball was touched down and there make a mark on the goal line and then walk straight out with it at right angles to the goal line such distance as he thinks proper and their place it for another of his side to kick. The kicker's side must be behind the ball when it is kicked, and the opposite side must remain behind their goal line until the ball has been placed on the ground (see Rules 54 and 55).

Rule 48: If the ball has been touched down between the goalposts, it may be brought out in a straight line from either of such posts but if brought out from between them the opposite may charge at once (see Rule 54).

Rule 49: If the try at goal be by a punt out (see Rule 29) a player of the side which has touched the ball down shall bring it straight up to the goal line opposite to the spot where it was touched down and there make a mark on the goal line and then punt out from any spot behind the goal line not nearer to the goalpost than such mark, or from touch in-goal if necessary, beyond which mark it is not lawful for the opposite side who must keep behind their goal line to pass until ball has been kicked (see Rules 54 and 55).

Rule 50: It a fair catch be made from a punt out or a punt on the catcher may either proceed as provided by Rules 43 and 44 or himself take a punt on in which case the mark made on making a fair catch shall be regarded (for the purpose of determining as well the position of the player who makes the punt on as of the other players of both sides) as the mark made on the goal line in the case of a punt out.

Rule 51: A catch made in touch from a punt out or a punt on is not a fair catch: the ball must then be taken or thrown out of touch as provided by Rule 32 but if the catch be made in touch in-goal the ball is at once dead and must be kicked out as provided by Rule 21.

Rule 52: When the ball has been touched down in the opponents' goal none of the side in whose goal it has been so touched down shall touch it or in any way displace it or interfere with the player of the other side who may be taking it up or out.

Rule 53: The ball is dead whenever a goal has been obtained, but if a try at goal be not successful the kick shall be considered as only an ordinary kick in the course of the game.

Rule 54: Charging i.e. rushing forward to kick the ball or tackle a player, is lawful for the opposite side in all cases of a place kick after a fair catch or upon a try at goal immediately the Ball touches or is placed on the ground; and in cases of a drop kick or punt after a fair catch as soon as the player having the ball commences to run or offers to kick or the ball has touched the ground but he may always draw back and unless he has dropped the ball or actually touched it with his foot they must again retire to his mark (see rule 56). The opposite side in the case of a punt out or a punt on, and the kicker's side in all cases may not charge until the ball has been kicked.

Rule 55: If a player having the ball when about to punt it out goes out side the goal line or when about to punt on advances nearer to his own goal line than his mark made on making the fair catch, or if after the ball has been touched down in the opponents' goal or a fair catch has been made more than one player on the side which has so touched it down or made the fair catch, touch the ball before it is again kicked the opposite side may charge at once.

Rule 56: In cases of a fair catch the opposite side may come up to and stand anywhere on or behind a line drawn through the mark made by the player who has made the catch and parallel to their own goal line; but in the case of a fair catch from a punt out or a punt on they may not advance further in the direction of the touch-line nearest to such mark than a line drawn through such mark to their goal line and parallel to such touch-line. In all cases (except a punt out and a punt on) the kicker's side must be behind the ball when it is kicked but may not charge until it has been kicked.

Rule 57: No hacking or hacking over or tripping up shall be allowed under any circumstances.

Rule 58: No one wearing projecting nails iron plates or gutta percha on any part of his boots or shoes shall be allowed to play in a match.

Rule 59: The captains of the respective sides shall be the sole arbiters of all disputes.

HOCKEY IN 1776

Finally, I present the rules of hockey as published in the 1776 book *Juvenile Sports and Pastimes* by Richard Johnson. I consider this a "non-connection" to organized hockey because the game at this time really cannot be called organized. Although it had some basic rules, it was much more of a pastime than a dedicated pursuit. However, as this is the earliest known set of printed rules for any kind of game called hockey, it is interesting in and of itself. It contains the first contemporary use of the word hockey, and the first known illustration of the game. And since this book was published in London, it is very likely that a game such as this ultimately led to the development of the Hockey Association rules discussed in Chapter 3.

Note that this passage refers to "new improvements" in the game of hockey, indicating that it had been played before this time. Also note that in this case, the object of pursuit, rather than the sticks themselves, is referred to as "the hockey." Here I reproduce only the parts of the passage relating to playing the game, and omit the author's personal thoughts on it.

New Improvements on the Game of Hockey

This is a noble and manly exercise, but is proper only for the cooler months of the year, as it requires a great share of activity. It was undoubtedly first taken from the Irish game of Hurling, which it resembles in almost every respect.

The materials for this sport are only of three sorts; the goals, the hockey, and the hockey-sticks, all which are easily to be procured, and without much expence [sic]...

This sport can be pursued no where with pleasure, but in a wide spacious field, where the hockey may have its full scope. This game may be played by any even number of boys, divided into two parties. Each party must fix their goal at the greatest distance from one another the field will admit of, leaving however about ten feet space between each goal and the extremity of the field. The goals need consist of only a very long piece of briar each end being stick in the ground, and thereby forming a kind of erect arch. The goal at the upper end on the field is called the upper goal, and the other the power: the parties who play are likewise distinguished in the same manner.

Every one who plays must be provided with a hockey-stick...I will give you the description of a good hockey-stick. It is no matter what wood it is, so that it is though, not liable to break, and has the desired form. It must be about a yard long, or rather in proportion to the size of the sportsman. The top of it, I mean that part of it which you hold in your hand, may be as thick as a common walking-stick; but the thicker it is at the bottom the better. The bottom, however, must not be strait [sic], but crooked, and that in the in the form of a shepherd's crook is valuable beyond everything. The use of the crook part is to disengage the hockey from your antagonists, when it is so surrounded by them that you cannot get at it to give it a full stroke toward their goal.

The kockey [sic] must be made of the largest cork-bung you can get. Cut the edges round, and then it is prepared for use.

188

The goals being fixed, the hockey prepared, and the parties agreed on, you then proceed to your sport in the following manner. Both parties meet as nearly as possible, in the middle between the two goals, when the hockey is tossed up, and every one tries his best to beat the hockey through the goal of his antagonist; which being once accomplished, the game is over.

...

According to the rules of the game, you are never to touch the kockey [sic] with your hands, from the time it is tossed up till it is got through one of the goals; and tho' you are allowed to push either of your antagonists aside, yet it is considered not only as foul play, but as very ungenteel also, to strive either to throw another down, or trip up his heels. Such proceedings always produce ill-will, quarrelling, and sometimes fighting: but every young gentleman will wish to make his companion as happy as himself, since, without mutual harmony, the finest sport in the world will be rendered dull, insipid, and disgustful [sic].

REFERENCES

Allen. Kevin (1998). "The Origins of American Hockey." In Diamond, Dan (ed.) *Total Hockey*. New York: Total Sports Publishing.

Arlott, John (Ed.) (1977). "Hockey, Field." In *The Oxford Companion to Sports and Games*. Frogmore, UK: Granada Publishing Limited.

Bodleian Library (2010). *The Original Rules of Rugby*. Oxford: Bodleian Library.

Boileau, Ron and Philip Wolf (2000). "The Pacific Coast Hockey Association." In Diamond, Dan (ed.) *Total Hockey (2nd Ed)*. New York: Total Sports Publishing.

Bowlsby, Craig H. (2006). *The Knights of Winter: Hockey in British Columbia 1895-1911*. Vancouver.

Channon, A. (2012). "Field Hockey, United Kingdom." In J. Nauright & C. Parrish (eds.) *Sports Around the World: History, Culture, and Practice*, vol. 2.

Coleman, Charles (1966). *The Trail of the Stanley Cup, Vol. 1, 1893-1926 Inc*. Montreal: National Hockey League.

Durand, Marc (2012). *La Coupe a Quebec: Les Bulldogs et la Naissance du Hockey*. Quebec: Editions Sylvain Harvey.

Farrell, Arthur (1899). *Hockey: Canada's Royal Winter Game*. Montreal: C.R. Corneil.

Fitsell, J.W. (2001). "The Halifax Rules: Fact or Fiction?" *Hockey Research Journal*, Vol. V, pp. 9-11.

Fitsell, J.W. (2006). *How Hockey Happened*. Kingston: Quarry Press Inc.

Johnson, Richard (1776). *Juvenile Sports and Pastimes* (2nd edition). London: T. Carnan, pp. 91-96.

Kitchen, Paul (2000). "Before the Trail of the Stanley Cup." In Diamond, Dan (ed.) *Total Hockey (Second Edition)*. New York: Total Sports Publishing.

Miroy, Nevill (1986). *The History of Hockey*. Laleham-on-Thames, UK: Lifeline Ltd.

Slater, Kevin (2010). *Season in Review Western Pennsylvania Hockey League 1899*. Blurb.com.

Slater, Kevin (2012). *Seasons in Review Hockey in Ontario 1883 – 1890*. Blurb.com.

Slater, Kevin (2012a). *Season in Review Ontario Hockey Association 1891 – 1892*. Blurb.com.

Smith, J. Nicholson and Philip A. Robson (1899). *Hockey Historical and Practical*. London: A.D. Innes & Company Limited.

Vigeault, Michel (2001). *La naissance d'un sport organise au Canada: le hockey a Montreal, 1875-1917*. Unpublished doctoral dissertation, Universite Laval, Quebec.

Young, Scott (1989). *100 Years of Dropping the Puck: A History of the OHA*. Toronto: McClelland & Stewart Inc.

Zuckerman, Earl (2000). "McGill University: The Missing Link to the Birthplace of Hockey." In Diamond, Dan (ed.) *Total Hockey (Second Edition)*. New York: Total Sports Publishing.

www.ingramcontent.com/pod-product-compliance
Lightning Source LLC
Chambersburg PA
CBHW022008100426
42736CB00041B/1089